SELF-PACED PHONICS
A Text for Educators

Fourth Edition

Roger S. Dow
Frostburg State University

G. Thomas Baer
Illinois State University

PEARSON

Merrill
Prentice Hall

Upper Saddle River, New Jersey
Columbus, Ohio

Library of Congress Cataloging-in-Publication Data

Dow, Roger S.
   Self-paced phonics: a text for educators/Roger S. Dow, G. Thomas Baer.—4th ed.
   p. cm.
   Includes bibliographical references.
   ISBN 0-13-227242-3
   1. Reading—Phonetic method. 2. Reading (Elementary) I. Baer, G. Thomas. II. Title.
   LB1573.3.B34 2007
   372.46'5—dc22

2006043827

Vice President and Executive Publisher: Jeffery W. Johnston
Senior Editor: Linda Ashe Bishop
Senior Production Editor: Mary M. Irvin
Design Coordinator: Diane C. Lorenzo
Senior Editorial Assistant: Laura Weaver
Production Coordination and Text Design: Lea Baranowski, Carlisle Editorial Services
Cover Designer: Jason Moore
Cover Image: Corbis
Production Manager: Pamela D. Bennett
Director of Marketing: David Gesell
Marketing Manager: Darcy Betts Prybella
Marketing Coordinator: Brian Mounts

This book was set in Palatino by Carlisle Publishing Services. It was printed and bound by
R. R. Donnelley & Sons Company. The cover was printed by Phoenix Color Corp.

Pearson Education Ltd.
Pearson Education Singapore Pte. Ltd.
Pearson Education Canada, Ltd.
Pearson Education—Japan

Pearson Education Australia Pty. Limited
Pearson Education North Asia Ltd.
Pearson Education de Mexico, S.A. de C.V.
Pearson Education Malaysia Pte. Ltd.

11 10 9 8
ISBN: 0-13-227242-3

PREFACE

Although phonics has been with us in one form or another from colonial times to the present, it continues to head the list of reading topics that elicit the most emotional responses—not only from detractors within the teaching profession but also from without. Based on the conclusions of reports such as *Becoming a Nation of Readers: The Report of the Commission of Reading* (Anderson et al., 1984) and *Beginning to Read: Thinking and Learning About Print* (Adams, 1990), there is strong evidence to suggest that children who are taught phonics at the beginning stages of reading instruction do better than those who are not. Clearly, the question regarding phonics instruction no longer appears to be whether it should be included in beginning instruction; instead, the essential question is one of determining how phonics can be taught most effectively.

The purpose of this text is to provide pre-service and practicing teachers with instruction that will assist them in developing a sound understanding of both the content and the pedagogy of phonics. This instruction is accomplished through the following text features and concepts:

Meaningful practice and feedback.

- The text uses sound learning principles by providing students with meaningful practice and immediate feedback. The chapter practices, cumulative reviews, pretest, and post-test provide students with numerous opportunities to work with the content of phonics. The coded pretest will assist learners in locating relevant material in the text, speeding mastery of the material.

Self-regulating, self-monitoring learning.

- Educators will be able to complete the text with a minimal amount of direct instruction. With little formal instruction required, faculty who already face content overload will find the text teacher friendly and immediately applicable to Web-based instructional models.

Complementary to reading methods.

- The text is designed to complement developmental reading methods textbooks that typically cover phonics in a superficial manner.

Phonics instruction in context.

- The text recognizes that, although phonics is only *one* of several word recognition techniques, it remains the one that is least understood by practicing and prospective teachers.

Input from students who have used the text over the past six years—along with evaluative feedback from reading professionals in the field—has been used to expand and strengthen the second and third editions of this text. The fourth edition includes Web links for further exploration of phonics-related topics. It also includes a source for standard pronunciation and additional information on many of the topics included in the text. This edition includes more examples that illustrate particular phonics elements and expands significantly the practices and cumulative reviews so that they provide increased opportunities for students to work with both the content and the pedagogy of phonics.

ACKNOWLEDGMENTS

Many thanks to the reviewers of this text for their insights and comments: Virginia McCormack, Ohio Dominican University; Karen M. Samson, Chicago State University; Marian Alice Simmons, University of Missouri-Kansas City; Alayne Sullivan, California State, San Bernardino; and the students in the Graduate Reading Program at Frostburg State University. Their countless suggestions and thorough discussion of this text were invaluable.

Teacher Preparation Classroom

See a demo at
www.prenhall.com/teacherprep/demo

TEACHER PREP

MERRILL
PRENTICE HALL

Your Class. Their Careers. Our Future. Will your students be prepared?

We invite you to explore our new, innovative and engaging website and all that it has to offer you, your course, and tomorrow's educators! Organized around the major courses pre-service teachers take, the Teacher Preparation site provides media, student/teacher artifacts, strategies, research articles, and other resources to equip your students with the quality tools needed to excel in their courses and prepare them for their first classroom.

This ultimate on-line education resource is available at no cost, when packaged with a Merrill text, and will provide you and your students access to:

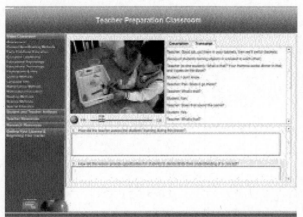

Online Video Library. More than 150 video clips—each tied to a course topic and framed by learning goals and Praxis-type questions—capture real teachers and students working in real classrooms, as well as in-depth interviews with both students and educators.

Student and Teacher Artifacts. More than 200 student and teacher classroom artifacts—each tied to a course topic and framed by learning goals and application questions—provide a wealth of materials and experiences to help make your study to become a professional teacher more concrete and hands-on.

Research Articles. Over 500 articles from ASCD's renowned journal *Educational Leadership*. The site also includes Research Navigator, a searchable database of additional educational journals.

Teaching Strategies. Over 500 strategies and lesson plans for you to use when you become a practicing professional.

Licensure and Career Tools. Resources devoted to helping you pass your licensure exam; learn standards, law, and public policies; plan a teaching portfolio; and succeed in your first year of teaching.

How to ORDER Teacher Prep for you and your students:
For students to receive a Teacher Prep Access Code with this text, instructors **must** provide a special value pack ISBN number on their textbook order form. To receive this special ISBN, please email **Merrill.marketing@pearsoned.com** and provide the following information:
  • Name and Affiliation
  • Author/Title/Edition of Merrill text
Upon ordering *Teacher Prep* for their students, instructors will be given a lifetime *Teacher Prep* Access Code.

CONTENTS

1 | INTRODUCTION

Phonics instruction has long been a controversial matter. Emans (1968) points out that the emphasis on phonics instruction has changed several times over the past two centuries. Instruction has shifted from one extreme—no phonics instruction—to the other extreme—phonics instruction as the major method of word-recognition instruction—and back again. Emans (1968) also points out that "each time that phonics has been returned to the classroom, it usually has been revised into something quite different from what it was when it was discarded" (p. 607). Currently, most beginning reading programs include a significant component of phonics instruction. This is especially true since the implementation of policies related to the No Child Left Behind Act and recommendations by the National Reading Panel for the use of instructional methods of both instruction and assessments related to explicit phonics instruction.

Phonics, however, is not the cure-all for reading ills that some believe it to be. Rudolph Flesch's book *Why Johnny Can't Read* (1955), although it did bring the phonics debate to the attention of the public, typifies the kind of literature that takes a naive approach to a very complex problem. As Heilman (1981) points out, "Flesch's suggestions for teaching were quite primitive, consisting primarily of lists of words each presenting different letter-sound patterns. Thus, Flesch did not actually provide teaching materials that schools and teachers could use" (p. 3). Still, this kind of approach, which reduced learning to read to the simple task of memorizing the alphabet and learning its letter-to-sound correspondences through an emphasis on writing, attracted disciples who vigorously carried forth its message.

Teachers must remember that phonics is but one of the major word-recognition methods that also include whole-word methodology and is most effective when it includes skills of contextual analysis, structural analysis, and dictionary use. These methods do not conflict with one another. If one is a proponent of phonics instruction, one does not have to be opposed to learning words via other word-recognition methods. Rather, it should be the goal of reading teachers to develop children's skills in all these methods for three basic reasons:

1. Children will find some methods more suited to their abilities and learning styles than others. Research has consistently shown that no one method is best for teaching all children. Thus, each child should be given opportunities to learn and use all word-recognition methods, applying those that work the most effectively for them.

2. Some words are learned more easily by using one method instead of another. For example, it may be more effective to teach an irregularly spelled word through a whole-word emphasis rather than a phonics emphasis. For example, focusing on word histories—the etymology of difficult words adopted from foreign languages—allows the learner to make deeper connections between the unique usage of the word and its irregular spelling.

3. When children encounter unknown words, they often use the various word-recognition techniques in concert, not as isolated skills having no relationship to one another.

Over the past 35 years, several studies and reports on reading stand out as having made major impacts on present-day phonics instruction. The first-grade reading studies (Bond & Dykstra, 1967) completed during the 1964–1965 school year provided data that have had an important and lasting influence on today's reading materials. Although the data seemed to indicate that no one method of teaching reading was superior to all others, they did suggest that an earlier and increased emphasis on phonics instruction would strengthen basal reading programs.

After an extensive critical analysis of research that examined the various approaches to beginning reading, Chall (1967) came to the following conclusions:

> My review of the research from the laboratory, the classroom, and the clinic points to the need for a correction in beginning reading instructional methods. Most schoolchildren in the United States are taught to read by what I have termed a meaning emphasis method. Yet, the research from 1912 to 1965 indicates that a code-emphasis method—i.e., one that views beginning reading as essentially different from mature reading and emphasizes learning of the printed code for the spoken language—produces better results, at least up to the point where sufficient evidence seems to be available, the end of the third grade.
>
> The results are better, not only in terms of the mechanical aspects of literacy alone, as was once supposed, but also in terms of the ultimate goals of reading instruction—comprehension and possibly even speed of reading. The long-existing fear that an initial code emphasis produces readers who do not read for meaning or with enjoyment is unfounded. On the contrary, the evidence indicates that better results in terms of reading for meaning are achieved with the programs that emphasize code at the start than with the programs that stress meaning at the beginning. (p. 307)

The National Academy of Education's Commission on Education and Public Policy, with the sponsorship of the National Institute of Education, established the Commission on Reading in 1983 to "locate topics on which there has been appreciable research and scholarship . . . and gather panels of experts from within the Academy and elsewhere to survey, interpret and synthesize research findings" (Anderson, Hiebert, Scott, & Wilkinson, 1984, p. viii). The Commission on Reading's efforts resulted in the influential report titled *Becoming a Nation of Readers*. In the foreword to this report, Robert Glaser, president of the National Academy of Education, writes,

> The last two decades of research and scholarship on reading, building on the past, have produced an array of information which is unparalleled in its

understanding of the underlying processes in the comprehension of language. Although reading abilities and disabilities require further investigation, present knowledge, combined with the centrality of literacy in the educational process, make the report cause for optimism. Gains from reading research demonstrate the power of new spectra of research findings and methodologies to account for the cognitive activities entailed in school learning. And because, in the schools and classrooms across the country, reading is an essential tool for success, we can hope for significant advances in academic achievement as the policies and practices outlined in these pages become more widespread. (Anderson et al., 1984, p. viii)

The Commission on Reading concluded that phonics instruction should hold an important place in beginning reading instruction and recommended that "teachers of beginning reading should present well-designed phonics instruction" (Anderson et al., 1984, p. 118).

In work supported by the U.S. Department of Education Cooperative Agreement with the Reading Research and Education Center of the University of Illinois at Urbana-Champaign, Marilyn J. Adams's work *Beginning to Read: Thinking and Learning About Print* has extended our understanding and knowledge on the issue of phonics and its role in learning to read. After an exhaustive review of pertinent basic and applied research, Adams (1990) concludes,

> In summary, deep and thorough knowledge of letters, spelling patterns, and words, and of the phonological translations of all three, are of inescapable importance to both skillful reading and its acquisition. By extension, instruction designed to develop children's sensitivity to spellings and their relations to pronunciations should be of paramount importance in the development of reading skills. This is, of course, precisely what is intended of good phonic instruction. (p. 416)

More recently, the National Reading Council's *Preventing Reading Difficulties in Young Children* (Snow, Burns, & Griffin, 1998) and the National Reading Panel's (NRP's) *Teaching Children to Read: An Evidence-Based Assessment of the Scientific Research on Reading and Its Implications for Reading Instruction* (National Institute of Child Health and Human Development, 2000a) provide further support for the importance of phonics in reading instruction. The NRP examined the research literature and concluded that

> the meta-analysis revealed that systematic phonics instruction produces significant benefits for students in kindergarten through 6th grade and for children having difficulty learning to read. (p. 9)

Hence, the question regarding phonics instruction no longer appears to be whether it should be included in beginning instruction. Instead, the essential question is one of determining how phonics can be taught most effectively. To assist teachers in teaching phonics effectively, several basic principles should underlie their actions:

1. Phonics must be viewed as a means to an end, not an end in itself. The purpose of phonics is to assist children in systematically decoding words that are unknown to them by teaching them the relationships that exist between letters and speech sounds.

2. Phonics will not work for all children. As with other methods of teaching reading, its effectiveness will run the gamut from ineffective to extremely effective. A challenge for teachers is to determine the proper match between phonics and the individual child and his or her learning style.

3. Phonics helps only if the unknown word is part of the reader's speaking-listening vocabulary. This is why it is very important to encourage parents and other caregivers to read aloud daily to beginning readers and provide them with guidance in learning not only the pronunciation of new words but their meanings as well. Take, for instance, the sentence "The boy ran to the sliet." Although you can venture a guess about the proper pronunciation of *sliet,* you have no way of knowing whether you are correct because it is a nonsense word and not part of your speaking-listening vocabulary.

4. Phonics is a skill that must be used in conjunction with the skills of contextual and structural analysis. Smith (1982) identifies the relationship between phonics and context:

> Phonic strategies cannot be expected to eliminate all the uncertainty when the reader has no idea what the word might be. But if the reader can reduce alternatives in advance—by making use of non-visual information related both to reading and to the subject matter of the text—then phonics can be made most efficient. One way to reduce uncertainty in advance is to employ the mediating technique of making use of context. (p. 147)

5. In learning phonics, children must have the opportunity to see, hear, and say the components they are asked to learn. Initial instruction and practice in phonics should, therefore, concentrate on oral activities. To accomplish this goal, teachers need to model continually the correct sounds of letters and words, and children need numerous opportunities to say these sounds and words. It is also important that teachers adhere to a standard of pronunciation that makes learning the sounds of the language consistent, avoiding dialectical markers that might inhibit student learning. It should be kept in mind that too many teaching materials require students to learn and/or practice phonics in a silent—and therefore ineffective—manner through the use of workbooks and other paper-and-pencil activities.

6. Phonics can be taught by using synthetic (explicit) and/or analytic (implicit) approaches to instruction. Although it must be understood that there is more than one significant difference between the synthetic and analytic approaches to phonics, the most basic difference between the two should be noted. Synthetic programs generally emphasize the learning of individual sounds, often in isolation, and follow with instruction that teaches children how to blend these individual sounds to form words (a part-to-whole approach). For instance, in the word *bat,* children would first sound out the isolated sounds (/b/ buh, /ă/ ah, /t/ tuh) and then blend them together to pronounce *bat.* Analytic programs, on the other hand, begin with whole words and identify individual sounds as part of those words. Teaching reading by starting with a whole word is a top-down approach because frequently the

focus of instruction is on the meaning of the word, not on its constituent sounds. Efforts are made to avoid pronouncing letter sounds in isolation (a whole-to-part approach). On this point, the Commission on Reading (Anderson et al., 1984) writes,

> In the judgment of the Commission, isolating the sounds associated with most letters and teaching children to blend the sounds of letters together to try to identify words are useful instructional strategies. These are the strategies of explicit phonics. However, research provides insufficient justification for strict adherence to either overall philosophy. Probably, the best strategy would draw from both approaches. (p. 42)

In *Beginning to Read: Thinking and Learning About Print—A Summary*, Stahl, Osborn, and Lehr (1990) recommend the use of explicit instruction in phonics:

> Because most phonemes cannot be pronounced without a vowel, many programs avoid or limit the use of isolated phonemes in their instruction. This practice often leads to potentially confusing instruction. The advantages of asking students to articulate phonemes in isolation outweigh the disadvantages.
>
> As you will learn later in the text, phonemes are the basic sounds that make up words in a language. Because beginning readers frequently have difficulty analyzing the sound structures of words, reading programs should include explicit instruction in blending. (p. 126)

The previously cited NRP report (2000a) further supports the inclusion of systematic synthetic phonics instruction:

> Systematic synthetic phonics instruction had a positive and significant effect on disabled readers' reading skills. These children improved substantially in their ability to read words and showed significant, albeit small, gains in their ability to process text as a result of systematic synthetic phonics instruction. This type of phonics instruction benefits both students with learning disabilities and low-achieving students who are not disabled. Moreover, systematic synthetic phonics instruction was significantly more effective in improving low socioeconomic status (SES) children's alphabetic knowledge and word reading skills than instructional approaches that were less focused on these initial reading skills. (p. 9)

7. "Phonics instruction should be kept simple and it should be completed by the end of second grade for most children" (Anderson et al., 1984, p. 118).

Through improved instruction, gains in reading achievement will be realized. Yet it has become painfully clear that too many teachers received inadequate emphasis on phonics in pre-service course work and lack basic knowledge that would allow them to present well-conceived and effective phonics instruction and be confident of its outcome for the learner.

The following chapters are designed to overcome this limiting factor by providing prospective teachers with a phonics knowledge base and teaching strategies that support it. Both will help teachers provide beginning readers with programs based on well-established principles of effective reading instruction.

CHAPTER 1: PRACTICE

1. Phonics (is, is not) the single most important factor in reading success. (Circle one.)

2. For most children, phonics instruction should be completed by the end of _____ grade.

3. Phonics is most effective when it is utilized with skills such as _____ and _____ analysis.

4. The purpose of phonics is to assist children in systematically decoding words that are unknown to them by teaching them the relationships that exist between _____ and _____.

5. Phonics programs that emphasize the learning of individual sounds, often in isolation, and follow with instruction that teaches children how to blend these individual sounds to form words are known as (analytic, synthetic) programs. (Circle one.)

6. (Analytic, Synthetic) phonics programs begin with whole words and identify individual sounds as parts of those words. (Circle one.)

7. Think back to your earliest school experiences. Visualize the methods by which you were taught to read. What role did phonics play?

   _____

   _____

   _____

8. Why is it instructionally ineffective to have children practice phonics by filling out workbook pages and ditto sheets?

   _____

   _____

   _____

   _____

   _____

   _____

   _____

   _____

9. Explain the following statement: "Phonics must be viewed as a means to an end, not an end in itself."

_____

_____

_____

_____

_____

_____

_____

_____

_____

10. Summarize the latest research as it relates to the use of systematic synthetic phonics instruction in beginning reading programs.

_____

_____

_____

_____

_____

_____

_____

_____

_____

For pronunciation standards and additional information regarding definitions used in this text, readers are encouraged to consult Merriam-Webster's online dictionary at http://www.m-w.com.

2 | PHONICS PRETEST

This pretest is designed to provide readers with feedback that should assist them in assessing their knowledge of phonics content. An analysis of results will help identify specific content problems and provide a focus as readers work through the text. Each question is coded for easy reference to the text location where additional information related to the content is found. Where itemized lists are cited, the page number and then the list number are cited. For example, "40.20" indicates the information is found on page 40 at list item number 20.

MATCHING

Match the words listed below with the appropriate definitions numbered 1 to 10.

a. phoneme   f. grapheme
b. digraph   g. macron
c. syllable   h. closed syllable
d. phonogram   i. consonant blend
e. phonics   j. diphthong

_____ 1. Two letters that stand for a single phoneme. (pp. 18, 53–54)

_____ 2. A letter or combination of letters that represents a phoneme. (p. 18)

_____ 3. Any syllable that ends with a consonant phoneme. (p. 19)

_____ 4. A method in which basic phonetics, the study of human speech sounds, is used to teach beginning reading. (p. 17)

_____ 5. The smallest *sound* unit of a language that distinguishes one word from another. (pp. 17, 19, 29–33)

_____ 6. A letter sequence comprised of a vowel grapheme and an ending consonant grapheme(s). (p. 19)

_____ 7. A *single vowel sound* made up of a blend of two vowel sounds in immediate sequence and pronounced in one syllable. (pp. 18, 48)

_____ 8. Sounds in a syllable represented by two or more letters that are blended together without losing their own identities. (pp. 17, 48–49)

_____ 9. A unit of pronunciation that consists of a vowel alone or a vowel with one or more consonants. (pp. 19, 44.2, 47)

_____ 10. The symbol placed over a vowel letter to show it is pronounced as a long sound. (p. 19)

TRUE–FALSE

_____ 11. The irregularity of vowel sounds is a basic problem of phonics. (pp. 48, 49)

_____ 12. The *schwa* sound is generally spelled in a consistent manner. (pp. 21, 61, 68)

_____ 13. Phonics is the most important skill required for effective reading. (pp. 1–5)

_____ 14. Synthetic phonics teaches students explicitly to convert letters into sounds and then blend the sounds to form recognizable words. (pp. 4–5)

_____ 15. A grapheme may be composed of one or more letters. (p. 17)

_____ 16. Each syllable must contain only one vowel letter. (pp. 19, 67–69)

_____ 17. In decoding multisyllabic words, syllabication should precede the application of vowel generalizations. (p. 67)

_____ 18. There are approximately 100 ways to spell the 44 phonemes. (pp. 19)

_____ 19. By the time the average child enters school, his or her auditory discrimination skills are fully developed. (pp. 36, 37)

_____ 20. The history of phonics shows that a phonics approach to teaching reading has been looked on favorably by most reading authorities over the past 50 years. (pp. iii, 1)

MULTIPLE CHOICE

_____ 21. Which of the following is a sound? (p. 17)
   a. grapheme
   b. vowel
   c. digraph
   d. none of the above

_____ 22. Which of the following words contains an open syllable? (p. 19)
   a. love
   b. son
   c. through
   d. fire

_____ 23. Which of the following words contains a digraph? (pp. 18, 47, 57, 58)
   a. fly
   b. bring
   c. blond
   d. home

_____ 24. Which of the following words contains letters that represent a diphthong? (pp. 18, 60)

    a. low
    b. meat
    c. through
    d. boy

_____ 25. How many phonemes are represented by the word *night*? (pp. 14, 42.25)

    a. 1
    b. 2
    c. 3
    d. 5

_____ 26. How many phonemes are represented by the word *boat*? (p. 18)

    a. 1
    b. 2
    c. 3
    d. 4

_____ 27. Which of the following pairs contains the same vowel phoneme? (p. 21)

    a. book—room
    b. too—shoe
    c. wool—food
    d. none of the above

_____ 28. Which of the following letters do not represent phonemes that are identified by their own name? (p. 20)

    a. t and s
    b. b and d
    c. y and z
    d. c and q

_____ 29. Which of the following consonant letters are most phonemically inconsistent in representing more than one sound? (pp. 20, 45.20, 47, 48, 56)

    a. b and d
    b. c and s
    c. r and t
    d. m and p

_____ 30. Which of the following letter pairs represents a consonant blend? (pp. 17, 57)

    a. ch
    b. br
    c. th
    d. -ng

_____ 31. Which of the following nonsense words would most likely represent the "soft c" sound? (pp. 45.22, 45.23, 47.1, 55, 56)

a. cint

b. cule

c. coble

d. calope

_____ 32. Which of the following nonsense words would most likely represent the "hard g" sound? (pp. 45.24, 47.2, 56)

a. giltion

b. seg

c. buge

d. gymp

_____ 33. Which of the following consonant letters affects the vowel that precedes it? (pp. 18, 44.5, 60)

a. m

b. t

c. r

d. none of the above

_____ 34. Which of the following words does not contain a consonant blend? (pp. 17, 57)

a. fruit

b. why

c. blue

d. flower

_____ 35. Which of the following words contains a closed syllable? (p. 19)

a. low

b. doubt

c. dough

d. boy

Circle the item in each list below that does not belong. Explain your reason for each.

36. sl   tr   bl   th   cl (pp. 17, 57, 58)

_____

_____

_____

37. sh   wh   st   ng   ch (pp. 57)

_____

_____

_____

38. a y i s w (pp. 20, 48, 55, 56)

_____

_____

_____

39. owl out low pound (pp. 18, 21, 48.4, 49.8, 58–60)

_____

_____

_____

40. gym gum game goat (pp. 47.2, 56)

_____

_____

_____

The following questions should be answered by using the vowel generalizations that are often taught in elementary schools. Each question requires the vowel pronunciation contained in a nonsense word.

_____ 41. The *a* in *kaic* has the same sound as that found in: (pp. 44.1, 44.6, 48.4, 58.3)

    a. art.
    b. may.
    c. map.
    d. None of the above.

_____ 42. The *e* in *clek* has the same sound as that found in: (pp. 18, 44.2, 58, 59)

    a. be.
    b. err.
    c. end.
    d. None of the above.

_____ 43. The *o* in *kote* has the same sound as that found in: (p. 44.4)

    a. not.
    b. or.
    c. go.
    d. boy.

_____ 44. The *a* in *psa* has the same sound as that found in: (pp. 19, 44.3, 48.2)

    a. art.
    b. may.
    c. map.
    d. None of the above.

_____ 45. The *i* in *sirp* has the same sound as that found in: (pp. 18, 49.7, 60)

   a. in.
   b. girl.
   c. high.
   d. None of the above.

_____ 46. The *a* in *woab* has the same sound as that found in: (pp. 44.1, 44.6, 48.4)

   a. art.
   b. may.
   c. map.
   d. None of the above.

_____ 47. The *u* in *kupp* has the same sound as that found in: (pp. 18, 44.2, 48.1)

   a. hurt.
   b. up.
   c. rude.
   d. None of the above.

_____ 48. The *u* in *nue* has the same sound as that found in: (p. 44.4)

   a. hurt.
   b. up.
   c. use.
   d. None of the above.

Indicate where the syllabic divisions occur in the following vowel-consonant letter patterns, nonsense words, or real words. Knowledge of syllabication generalizations is essential. There are no consonant digraphs in questions 49 through 52 (C = consonant letter, V = vowel letter). (p. 69.9)

_____ 49. CVCVCC (p. 69.9)

   a. CVC-VCC
   b. CV-CVCC
   c. CVCV-CC
   d. CV-CV-CC

_____ 50. CVCCVC (p. 69.8)

   a. CV-CCVC
   b. CVCC-VC
   c. CVC-CVC
   d. CV-CC-VC

_____ 51. CVCCV (p. 69.8)

   a. CVC-CV
   b. CV-CCV
   c. CVCC-V
   d. C-V-CCV

_____ 52. CCVCVCC (p. 68.1)

    a. CCVC-VCC
    b. CCV-C-VCC
    c. CC-VC-VCC
    d. CCV-CVCC

_____ 53. intayed (p. 68.2b)

    a. in-tay-ed
    b. in-tayed
    c. in-ta-yed
    d. intay-ed

_____ 54. makution (p. 68.2)

    a. ma-ku-tion
    b. mak-u-tion
    c. mak-u-ti-on
    d. ma-ku-ti-on

_____ 55. sleble (p. 68.4)

    a. sleb-le
    b. sleble
    c. sl-e-ble
    d. sle-ble

_____ 56. exanthema (p. 68.2)

    a. exan-the-ma
    b. ex-an-the-ma
    c. ex-an-them-a
    d. e-xan-the-ma

_____ 57. getker (p. 69.8)

    a. ge-tker
    b. get-ker
    c. getk-er
    d. getker

Reading programs often introduce long and short vowel sounds based on spelling patterns. In the following patterns (V = vowel letter; C = consonant letter), indicate which vowel sound you would expect the pattern to represent (L = long sound; S = short sound).

_____ 58. VC (pp. 18, 47.43)
_____ 59. VCe (_e_ = final _e_ in word) (p. 44.4)
_____ 60. CVCC (p. 44.2)
_____ 61. CV (p. 44.3)

CHAPTER 2: PRACTICE

Check your answers against those listed in Appendix A. If you had difficulty, don't be discouraged. Rather, analyze your results to identify areas that gave

you the most trouble. List these problem areas below. As you work through
the text, use this information to provide a focus for your study.

_____

_____

_____

_____

_____

_____

_____

_____

_____

_____

CUMULATIVE REVIEW: CHAPTERS 1 AND 2

1. The major word-recognition methods include phonics, whole-word methodology, _____, _____, _____, _____, and dictionary use.

2. Generally, the phonics instruction that appeared 35 years ago (is, is not) the same as that taught today. (Circle one.)

3. There (are, are not) significant research data that show the importance of phonics in beginning reading instruction. (Circle one.)

4. According to the latest research, the advantages of systematic synthetic phonics instruction (outweigh, do not outweigh) the disadvantages. (Circle one.)

5. Over the past 50 years, using a phonics approach to teaching beginning reading (has, has not) been consistently looked on favorably by most reading authorities. (Circle one.)

6. Learning letter sounds in isolation and blending them together to form words is an example of (synthetic, analytic) phonics. (Circle one.)

7. Why do most authorities suggest that phonics instruction be completed by the end of second grade for most children?

_____

_____

_____

_____

_____

_____

8. Explain the difference between explicit (synthetic) phonics instruction and implicit (analytic) phonics instruction.

_____

_____

_____

_____

_____

_____

9. From what you know about the whole-language philosophy, do you believe it is compatible with the teaching of phonics? Explain.

_____

_____

_____

_____

_____

10. If an unknown word is not part of a reader's speaking-listening vocabulary, why will phonics be of little value in the process of decoding?

_____

_____

_____

_____

_____

3 PHONICS VOCABULARY AND PHONEMES

VOCABULARY

Although a more detailed glossary appears at the end of this text (see the Glossary on page 117), an introduction of pertinent vocabulary at this juncture will assist readers of this text. Ultimately, the following vocabulary words should be learned to the point where all meanings are understood instantly (a state known as *automaticity*). Related terms are grouped together.

phonics: A method in which basic phonetics, the study of human speech sounds, is used to teach beginning reading. Teachers teach phonics, not phonetics.

phonetics: The study of human speech sounds.

phoneme: The smallest *sound* unit of a language that distinguishes one word from another. Examples: the phoneme /h/ distinguishes *hat* from *at;* the words *tell* and *yell* are distinguished by their initial phonemes /t/ and /y/. (This text indicates that there are 44 phonemes in the American-English language. This number varies, however, according to different authorities and/or dialects. Slash marks, //, are used throughout the text to indicate that the reference is to a *sound* and not a *letter.*)

phonemic awareness: The ability to recognize spoken words as a sequence of individual sounds.

consonant: A sound represented by any letter of the English alphabet except *a, e, i, o, u.* Consonants are sounds made by closing or restricting the breath channel.

consonant blend: Sounds in a syllable represented by two or more letters that are blended together without losing their own identities. Examples: *bl*ue /b/ /l/; *gr*ay /g/ /r/; *br*own /b/ /r/; *tw*ig /t/ /w/; *str*eet /s/ /t/ /r/; *fl*ip /f/ /l/.

vowel: A sound represented by *a, e, i, o, u* and sometimes *y* and *w* in the English alphabet. Vowels are sounds made without closing or restricting the breath channel. Saying the names of the vowels out loud will cause your vocal cords to vibrate.

This characteristic of sounds is called *voicing* and helps beginning readers to hear distinctions between sounds. Vowels that record their long sounds when said aloud are always voiced. It is important to understand that speech sounds are categorized by where they are produced in the vocal system. The tongue, palate, the uvula (the little flap of tissue at the rear of your mouth), and your teeth all influence the way sounds are produced. As you will see later, the place of articulation within the vocal mechanism determines how speech sounds are coded by the use of various pronunciation guides called *diacritical marks.* Dictionaries standardize these pronunciations by providing pronunciation guides. Linguists categorize speech sounds according to where they are produced within the vocal mechanism.

diphthong: A single vowel sound made up of a glide from one vowel sound to another in immediate sequence and pronounced in one syllable. Examples: /oi/ in *oil* and b*oy*, /ou/ in h*ou*se, /ow/ in *owl*, and /ew/ in f*ew*. (Phonetics would consider that some single-letter vowels represent diphthongs. For the purposes of teaching reading, however, only /oi/ and /ou/ will be considered diphthongs.)

r-controlled vowel: When a vowel letter is followed by the letter *r*, it affects the vowel sound so that it is neither short nor long. For example, in *her,* the vowel sound becomes /û/; in *dare,* it becomes /â/; in *for,* it becomes /ô/; in *car,* it becomes /ä/.

schwa sound: An unstressed sound commonly occurring in unstressed syllables. It is represented by the symbol /ǝ/ and closely resembles the short sound for *u.* Examples: *a* in *about; o* in *occur; i* in *pencil; u* in *circus.* The schwa sound is the most common vowel sound in English and may be represented by any vowel letter.

grapheme: A letter or combination of letters that represents a phoneme (sound). Examples: the phoneme /b/ in *bat* is represented by the grapheme *b;* the phoneme /f/ in *phone* is represented by the grapheme *ph.* (There are over 200 different ways to spell the phonemes. For example, /f/ can take the form of *f* in *fine, gh* in *cough,* and *ph* in *elephant.* This is an example of three different graphemes representing the same phoneme.)

digraph: Two letters that stand for a single phoneme (sound). Examples: *th*in /th/; *each* /ē/; *sh*op /sh/; b*oy* /oi/; *look* /ŏŏ/; ra*ng* /ng/; f*ew* /o͞o/. A digraph is simply a grapheme of two letters.

onset: The consonant sound(s) of a syllable that come(s) before the vowel sound. (Examples are included with the definition of *rime* below.)

rime: The part of a syllable that includes the vowel sound and any consonant sound(s) that come(s) after it. The graphic representation of a rime is referred to as a *phonogram.* Following are examples of both onsets and rimes.

Word	Onset	Rime	Phonogram
mat	/m/	/at/	at
pig	/p/	/ig/	ig
at	—	/at/	at
split	/spl/	/it/	it

phonogram: A letter sequence comprised of a vowel grapheme and (an) ending consonant grapheme(s), such as *-ig* in *wig, dig, big* or the *-ack* in *back, tack, sack*. From phonograms, we can generate word families.

---

syllable: A unit of pronunciation consisting of a vowel alone or a vowel with one or more consonants. There can be only one vowel phoneme (sound) in each syllable.

closed syllable: Any syllable that ends with a consonant phoneme (sound). Examples: come /m/; paste /t/; love /v/; ran /n/.

open syllable: Any syllable that ends with a vowel sound (phoneme). Examples: see /ē/; may /ā/; boy /oi/; auto /ō/.

---

breve: The orthographic symbol (˘) placed over a vowel letter to show it is pronounced as a short sound (sometimes called an unglided vowel).

circumflex: The orthographic symbol (^) placed above vowel graphemes to indicate pronunciation.

macron: The orthographic symbol (−) placed over a vowel letter to show it is pronounced as a long sound (sometimes called a glided vowel).

umlaut: The orthographic symbol (¨) placed above vowel graphemes to indicate pronunciation.

PHONEMES

As previously defined, phonemes are the smallest sound units of a language that distinguish one word from another. There are 44 phonemes in the English language; 25 of these are consonant phonemes, and 19 are vowel phonemes. The fact that there are over 200 different ways to spell the 44 phonemes creates confusion when learning how to read or spell in English. It is helpful to realize that English is not a static language. Many of the so-called irregular pronunciations that appear not to conform to phonics generalizations occur because they are used frequently, are borrowed or adapted from other languages with different pronunciation patterns, or have changed as a function of time. It is worthwhile for teachers to study exceptions to the rules or generalizations of phonics since often this will assist them in explaining the exceptions to beginning readers.

Consonant Phonemes—Pronunciation Key

Single Letters (there are 18)
Each word below represents the most common spelling of an initial consonant sound.

/b/	bat
/d/	did
/f/	fat
/g/	go
/h/	he
/j/	jam
/k/	come
/l/	let
/m/	me
/n/	no
/p/	pan
/r/	run
/s/	sat
/t/	ten
/v/	very
/w/	will
/y/	yes
/z/	zoo

Letters *c, q,* and *x* do not represent phonemes that are identified by their own names. Instead, these sound units are identified with like-sounding phonemes from the list above:

c represents the phonemes we associate with /s/ in *cent* or /k/ in *coat.*

q represents the phonemes we associate with /k/ /w/ in *quit* or /k/ in *antique.*

x represents the phonemes we associate with /g/ /z/ in *exit,* /k/ /s/ in *sox,* or /z/ in *xylophone.*

Double Letters (there are 7)

/ch/	chair
/hw/	why
/ng/	song
/sh/	she
/th/	thin

/TH/	that
/zh/	measure

Vowel Phonemes—Pronunciation Key

Each word listed below represents the most common spelling of vowel phonemes.

Long Vowels

/ā/	age
/ē/	ease
/ī/	ice
/ō/	old
/ū/	use

Short Vowels

/ă/	an
/ĕ/	end
/ĭ/	in
/ŏ/	odd
/ŭ/	up

Diphthongs

/oi/	oil, boy
/ou/	out, owl
/ew/	few

Double o

/o͞o/	too, rule
/o͝o/	good, pudding

Others

/ä/	father, star
/â/	dare, air
/û/	her, pearl
/ô/	auto, off, order

When vowel letters are followed by an *r*, they are known as *r-controlled*. This results in a sound that is neither short nor long.

Schwa /ə/: A schwa is a short, unstressed vowel that often occurs in unaccented syllables. The sound that schwa presents in a word varies depending on the vowel it represents and/or the sounds surrounding it.

a as in *about, senator*

o as in *occur, lemon*

e as in *effect, open*

i as in *pencil, notify*

u as in *circus, insulate*

au as in *authority*

ai as in *mountain*

ou as in *famous*

ea as in *pageant*

eo as in *dungeon*

oi as in *tortoise*

CHAPTER 3: PRACTICE

1. Circle each of the following terms that refers to a sound:

   phoneme   vowel   grapheme   rime
   diphthong digraph   consonant   phonogram

2. Vowel sounds are usually represented by the following letters:
   _____, _____, _____,
   _____, and _____. Also, _____
   and _____ sometimes represent vowels.

3. Circle each of the following words that contains an open syllable:

   son   go   dew
   love   through   fire

4. A _____ is composed of two letters that stand for a single
   phoneme.

5. Underline any consonant digraph contained in the following words:

   blue   bring   the   street   shut   chill   train

6. Underline any vowel digraph contained in the following words:

   dew   look   love   soup   boy   go   beat

7. A _____ is a special *single* vowel sound made up of a glide from one vowel to another. The phonemes that represent these sounds are /oi/ and /_____/.

8. Each syllable must contain one and only one vowel _____.

9. The orthographic symbol used to represent a long vowel sound is called a _____.

10. The orthographic symbol used to represent a short vowel sound is called a _____.

11. The letters that represent a diphthong are called a _____.

12. A(n) _____ syllable ends with a consonant phoneme.

13. A special kind of grapheme that consists of two letters is called a _____.

14. The study of human speech sounds is known as _____.

15. There are _____ phonemes in the English language, _____ consonant phonemes, and _____ vowel phonemes.

16. The schwa sound usually has a(n) (consistent, inconsistent) spelling. (Circle one.)

17. The inconsistent spelling of (consonant sounds, vowel sounds) is a basic problem of phonics. (Circle one.)

18. Check the pair(s) below that contain(s) the same vowel phoneme.

    a. book—room _____
    b. wool—food _____
    c. pool—stood _____
    d. too—shoes _____

19. Check each word below that contains a diphthong.

    a. coil _____
    b. out _____
    c. own _____
    d. owl _____
    e. could _____

20. The letters _____, _____, and _____ do not represent phonemes that are identified by their own names.

21. Fill in the proper consonant phoneme for each of the underlined letter(s).

    center   /_____/   sei<u>z</u>ure   /_____/
    <u>ch</u>rome   /_____/   gra<u>ph</u>   /_____/

know	/_____/	germ	/_____/
sure	/_____/	whom	/_____/
wrong	/_____/	ghost	/_____/
white	/_____/	antique	/_____/

22. Fill in the proper vowel phoneme for each of the underlined letter(s).

paid	/_____/	turn	/_____/
die	/_____/	plaid	/_____/
boy	/_____/	owl	/_____/
eulogy	/_____/	pull	/_____/
wand	/_____/	said	/_____/
rule	/_____/	other	/_____/

23. How many phonemes are represented in the following words? Write each word using its phoneme pronunciation symbols.

sight	3	/s/ /ī/ /t/
sew	____	_____
sing	____	_____
blue	____	_____
ghost	____	_____
ship	____	_____
old	____	_____
boy	____	_____
bird	____	_____
both	____	_____
box	____	_____
cent	____	_____
comb	____	_____
cow	____	_____
low	____	_____

24. Define the following phonics terms. If you are able to define them in your own words, you are well on your way to internalizing them and achieving automaticity.

Vowel:

_____

_____

_____

Grapheme:

_____

_____

_____

Phoneme:

_____
_____
_____

Consonant:

_____
_____
_____

Syllable:

_____
_____
_____

Macron:

_____
_____
_____

Open Syllable:

_____
_____
_____

Breve:

_____
_____
_____

Digraph:

_____
_____
_____

Rime:

_____
_____
_____

CUMULATIVE REVIEW: CHAPTERS 1 TO 3

1. There (are, are not) sufficient research data that show that systematic phonics instruction produces significant benefits for students learning to read. (Circle one.)

2. Systematic synthetic phonics instruction (has, does not have) a positive and significant effect on disabled readers' reading skills. (Circle one.)

3. Underline any letters in the following words that represent a consonant blend.

   that   she   blend   church   street   why   sing

4. Identify a word in which the letter *w* functions as a vowel.

   _____

5. (Synthetic, Analytic) programs generally emphasize the learning of individual sounds, often in isolation, and follow with instruction that teaches children how to blend these individual sounds to form words. (Circle one.)

6. (Synthetic, Analytic) programs begin with whole words and identify individual sounds as part of those words. Efforts are made to avoid pronouncing letter sounds in isolation. (Circle one.)

7. What is the relationship between phonics and a person's speaking–listening vocabulary?

   _____

   _____

   _____

   _____

   _____

   _____

8. A (phonics, whole-word) emphasis would most likely be more effective with a word such as *pneumonia*. (Circle one.) Why?

   _____

   _____

   _____

_____

_____

9. What are the differences between a digraph and diphthong?

_____

_____

_____

_____

_____

_____

_____

10. What is the difference between a consonant digraph and a consonant blend?

_____

_____

_____

_____

_____

_____

_____

11. What is the difference between a phonogram and a rime?

_____

_____

_____

_____

_____

_____

12. When the letter _r_ follows a vowel letter, how does it affect the vowel?

_____

_____

_____

_____

_____

_____

_____

13. How does knowledge of phonics foster independence in learning to read?

_____

_____

_____

_____

_____

_____

_____

Helpful Web addresses related to this chapter:

The International Phonetic Alphabet
http://www.omniglot.com/writing/ipa.htm
http://www.arts.gla.ac.uk/IPA/ipachart.html

4 EMERGENT LITERACY AND PHONICS

Although most attention to readiness factors has been placed in the context of formal schooling, the encounters that children have with reading and writing before formal schooling begins have become increasingly important in understanding how children learn to read. Sulzby and Teale (1991) explain emergent literacy as follows:

> Emergent literacy is concerned with the earliest phases of literacy development, the period between birth and the time when children read and write conventionally. The term *emergent literacy* signals a belief that, in a literate society, young children—even 1- and 2-year-olds—are in the process of becoming literate. This literacy is seen in not-yet-conventional behaviors; underlying the behaviors are understandings or hypotheses about literacy. Literacy learning is seen as taking place in home and community settings, in out-of-home care settings, and in school settings such as Head Start, pre-kindergarten, and kindergarten. (p. 728)

Thus, it is important for teachers to realize that the wide range of experiences that children have had with language before formal school begins should be used in assisting them to learn to read. Children's understanding about print awareness, concepts of print, sense of story, oral language, and writing will have a significant bearing on their ultimate success in reading achievement.

Many factors have been identified as having some influence on success in beginning reading. Intelligence, general health, vision, hearing, motor coordination, sex, listening ability, language development, auditory discrimination, visual discrimination, background experience, emotional adjustment, story sense, age, phonemic awareness, and knowledge of letter names head the list of factors that have been discussed in methods texts over the past 35 years (Harris & Smith, 1986; Searfoss & Readence, 1994; Spache & Spache, 1986). For the purposes of this text, only those factors relating most directly to a phonics approach to reading are discussed at length.

ORAL LANGUAGE

Research has shown that a positive relationship exists between oral language and reading achievement (Blackman, 1984; Edmiaston, 1984; Rosenthal, Baker, & Ginsburg, 1983). It appears that oral language serves as an essential foundation on which reading instruction can and should be built. Furthermore, the Russian psychologist Vygotsky (Flavell, 1977) believed that for young children to have thoughts, they must say them out loud. In essence, if Vygotsky was correct, to silence young children is to silence their thoughts. For this reason, teachers must understand the significance of oral language in beginning reading instruction and learning in general and to include activities in the curriculum that build on the language skills children bring to school.

Searfoss and Readence (1994) believe that the rationale for oral language instruction should be based on three key processes:

1. Oral-language programs should utilize real experiences children have both in and out of school.

2. Oral-language development should be viewed as an integral part of the whole school day, planned but arising from naturally occurring events in the classroom.

3. Oral-language (speaking and listening) activities should lead naturally into using the tools of reading and writing. Activities designed to develop oral language should be integrated with reading and writing (p. 63).

The following is a sampling of the kinds of classroom activities that can be used to accomplish effective oral language instruction.

Activity 1: Read to children often. This activity has a positive effect on language development and can have an impact on children's attitudes toward reading. The physical context of the reading event should be warm, nurturing, and supportive. Since parents and caregivers are typically intimately aware of the child's interests and prior knowledge, their selection of developmentally appropriate reading material is very important. Jim Trelease's (1995) book *The New Read-Aloud Handbook* is an excellent resource for both parents and educators in the identification and selection of books to be read aloud.

Activity 2: Each day, provide children with numerous opportunities to express themselves. To accomplish this, set up situations that allow students to share experiences, ask questions, develop stories to be shared with others, resolve problems through language, and express attitudes and feelings. When teachers spend time at the beginning of the school day in activities such as "show and tell" or "bring and brag," they provide children with appropriate opportunities to express themselves orally. Activities that promote sharing oral language provide the teacher with opportunities to expand the vocabularies of their students.

Activity 3: Use patterned books along with rhymes, poems, and songs to help develop children's oral language. Because these types of materials are very predictable, children can join quickly in the reading process.

Activity 4: Develop language-experience stories using the children's natural language. In this process, children use language to explore a common experience. Once this oral exploration is exhausted, the teacher tells the class that she would like to write a story about their experiences. Using the children's own language, the teacher takes dictation and writes out their story on a large chart-paper tablet, that is then used as reading material that children can begin to read. This procedure helps children come to understand that what can be said can be written down and preserved, to be used later through the act of reading.

PHONEMIC AWARENESS

The high correlation that exists between the ability to recognize spoken words as a sequence of individual sounds and reading achievement has been well established over the past 35 years (Bradley & Bryant, 1983; Calfee & Ehri, 1979; Golinkoff, 1978; Lindamood & Lindamood, 1973; Mann, 1994; Stuart, 1999; Tunmer & Nesdale, 1985). This correlation has generated interest in and research into the feasibility of teaching phonemic awareness to children at the kindergarten and first-grade levels. Lewkowicz (1980), in her analysis of 10 tasks that have been used by researchers or classroom teachers to test or teach phonemic awareness, came to the conclusion that two of these tasks, *segmentation* and *blending,* were basic and belonged in beginning instructional programs.

The reports of the Subgroups of the National Reading Panel *Teaching Children to Read* (National Institute of Child Health and Human Development, 2000b) indicate that phonemic awareness can be taught and does help children learn to read and spell:

> Results of the meta-analysis showed that teaching phonemic awareness to children is clearly effective. It improves their ability to manipulate phonemes in speech. This skill transfers and helps them learn to read and spell. PA [phonemic awareness] training benefits not only word reading but also reading comprehension. PA training contributes to children's ability to read and spell for months, if not years, after training has ended. Effects of PA training are enhanced when children are taught how to apply PA skills to reading and writing tasks. (pp. 2–40)

Teaching children to manipulate phonemes can be taught in a number of ways. Examples of activities appropriate at the readiness level (defined as kindergarten to first grade) follow:

Activity 1—Phoneme Isolation: Teach children to isolate sounds in words. This can be accomplished in several ways:

1. Teach children to hear and recognize initial sounds in words by prolonging or stretching pronunciation of initial sounds of words or iterating (repeating several times, especially the sounds recorded by vowels) the initial sounds of words.

2. Have children practice this skill by matching a sound with a picture of an object that represents that sound when read. For instance, say /b/ and have the children attempt to match it with a picture of a ball.

3. Have children practice identifying the initial sounds in words by reading words to them and asking them what sound each word starts with.

Activity 2—Phoneme Identity: Teach children to recognize common sounds in different words. For example, have them identify the sound that is the same in two words (*ball, boy*) and expand to three words (*ball, boy, bed*).

Activity 3—Phoneme Categorization: This activity requires children to recognize which word in a series of three or four words has a different sound (*ball, bed, cat*) (*ball, bed, boat, dog*).

Activity 4—Phoneme Counting: Ask children to count the number of sounds they hear as you read words slowly. Start with two-letter words and advance from there. Gradually reduce the slowness of pronunciation as children gain proficiency in this skill.

Activity 5—Phoneme Deletion: This activity requires children to identify a new word that is made when a phoneme is deleted from the original word. For example, they might be asked to say *sat* with the /s/ deleted. This activity may be more effective if the leftover words are also real words. Extending this activity to include ending and medial sounds should occur only after students become confident in their abilities to deal with beginning sounds.

Activity 6—Identification of Deleted Phonemes: This activity is similar to activity 5 because it relates to a deleted phoneme. In this activity, however, children are asked to identify the missing phoneme when comparing two similar sounding words. For instance, what sound do you hear in *mat* that is not in *at*?

Activity 7—Phoneme Substitution: Replace an identified sound with a new one and pronounce the new word. For instance, in the word *seat*, if you replace the /s/ with a /b/, how is the new word pronounced? (A similar activity is often used in which children are asked to identify new words through letter substitution rather than through sound substitution. It is suggested here that more work be done with sound substitutions.)

Activity 8—Phoneme Segmentation: Phoneme segmentation is the ability to isolate all the sounds of a word. Nation and Hulme (1997) found in their research that "phonemic segmentation is an excellent predictor of reading and spelling skill, even in the early stages of literacy development" (p. 166). In teaching this skill, Lewkowicz (1980) found that it is extremely important for the teacher to prolong or stretch the word to be segmented and essential that the child attend to the articulatory clues, as well as the auditory clues, by slowly pronouncing the word.

1. Introduce children to the concept through modeling: slowly saying a word and emphasizing its sounds, then identifying each sound separately. For instance, read *dog* slowly and then identify /d/ /ô/ /g/ as the word's three sounds.

2. Provide practice for children by slowly reading words to them, emphasizing each sound. Ask children to articulate the individual sounds that make up each word. Start with two-letter words and advance from there to longer words as children become competent in voicing each sound in the words. At

first, it is also effective to help students by identifying the number of sounds in each word. As students gain the ability to segment words, the number of sounds can be withheld.

Activity 9—Phoneme Blending: Blending is the process of recognizing isolated speech sounds and the ability to pronounce the word for which they stand when combined. The most appropriate time to "introduce blending seems likely to be when children have just 'gotten the hang of' segmentation and are practicing it intensively" (Lewkowicz, 1980, p. 697).

1. Have children practice blending two-phoneme words segmented into two parts (e.g., /n/ /ō/).

2. Have children practice blending three- or four-phoneme words segmented into two parts (e.g., /r/–/ă/ /t/; /s/ /t/–/ŏ/ /p/).

3. Advance to having children practice blending three- or four-phoneme words segmented into three parts (e.g., /d/–/ô/–/g/; /t/ /r/–/ĭ/–/p/.

Research seems to indicate, however, that focusing on one or two skills produces better results than focusing on many at the same time.

> Although all of the approaches exert a significant effect on reading, instruction that focuses on one or two skills produces greater transfer than a multi-skilled approach. Teaching students to segment and blend benefits reading more than a multi-skilled approach. Teaching students to manipulate phonemes with letters yields larger effects than teaching students without letters, not surprisingly because letters help children make the connection between phonemic awareness and its application to reading. Teaching children to blend the phonemes represented by letters is the equivalent of decoding instruction. Being explicit about the connection between phonemic awareness skills and reading also strengthens training effects. (National Institute of Child Health and Human Development, 2000b, pp. 2–41)

LETTER NAMES

To provide effective readiness instruction, teachers must understand the type of relationship that exists between knowledge of letter names and learning to read:

> A number of research studies have shown that letter knowledge is not necessarily a prerequisite for learning to read. On the other hand numerous studies have also shown that children who begin their schooling with knowledge of the ABC's are more likely to become better readers than children who lack this knowledge. For some time this was taken to mean that letter knowledge was helpful or necessary in learning to read. Most authorities now agree, however, that knowledge of the ABC's for entering school aged children is simply indicative of a host of factors that are often conducive to learning to read. Among these factors are a natural potential for learning to read, educational level of [the student's] parents, and [a] good reading environment at home. (Ekwall, 1976, p. 64)

Therefore, the readiness instruction in letter names for phonics must not be done under the false assumption that it will *cause* children to become good readers. Rather, it should be understood that children's knowledge of letter names will enable the teacher to communicate more effectively with them as instruction occurs.

VISION

Reading is a visual act that requires effective near-point (close) vision. Inadequate visual acuity may account for more than half of all reading failure (Shanker & Ekwall, 2003). Yet the types of tests often administered to children at the beginning stages of schooling simply measure far-point (distance) vision. Therefore, a cumulative file that contains information indicating that a child has successfully passed a vision test may be misleading. For this reason, teachers must be sensitive to signs in students that may indicate visual problems. Harris and Smith (1986) suggest that the following behaviors may be signs of visual problems:

1. Cocking the head to read with only one eye.
2. Holding the side of one's head when looking at the book or board.
3. Rubbing the eyes during reading.
4. Red eyes, watery eyes.
5. Holding the book too close to the face.
6. Holding the book at arm's length.
7. Complaints of headaches.
8. Squinting or other indications of strain.
9. Complaints of haziness or fading of printed symbols (p. 122).

HEARING

Auditory acuity, the ability to hear sounds of varying pitch and loudness, is an important factor in beginning reading. For instance, students who suffer hearing losses that affect their ability to hear high-frequency sounds may have difficulty in hearing certain consonants and consonant blends. Bond, Tinker, Wasson, and Wasson (1989) suggest that the following behaviors may be signs of auditory acuity problems:

1. Inattention during listening activities.
2. Frequent misunderstanding of oral directions or numerous requests for repetition of statements.
3. Turning one ear toward the speaker or thrusting head forward when listening.
4. Intent gaze at the speaker's face or strained posture while listening.

5. Monotone speech, poor pronunciation, or indistinct articulation.
6. Complaints of earache or hearing difficulty.
7. Insistence on closeness to sound sources.
8. Frequent colds, discharging ears, or difficult breathing (pp. 53–54).

If some of these behaviors are observed in students, they should serve as an alert that there may be a physical problem with either sight or vision that is hindering effective learning. If these behaviors continue after closer scrutiny, a referral should be made to an appropriate school official who has been trained to deal with these problems.

VISUAL DISCRIMINATION

Children develop their abilities to discriminate visually as they explore their environments through a combination of tactile and visual approaches. Spache and Spache (1986) point out that children who lack experiences with objects or forms at near-point range often have difficulty with reading.

Since reading is a visual act and requires visual discrimination ability, teachers should prepare children for phonics by providing exercises that help them discriminate between letters and words. Research results indicate that this task is best accomplished by having children practice using letters and words rather than pictures or various geometric shapes (Durkin, 1993).

Visual Discrimination Exercises

Visual discrimination exercises should progress in a logical sequence from simple to complex. Below are sequenced examples of exercises that can be used to further develop visual discrimination skills. Beyond these examples, teachers should be able to develop additional activities for improving visual discrimination.

Activity 1—Matching Letters: In this example, the student circles the letter on each line that is identical to the first letter of that line. (Examples progress from simple to complex.)

t	s	w	t	o
O	T	O	V	X
w	m	n	w	u
b	d	b	p	q

Activity 2—Matching Double Letters: In this example, the student circles the pair of letters on each line that is identical to the first two letters of that line. (Examples progress from simple to complex.)

ok	ts	xy	ok	mn
SP	OT	SP	MA	UW

ab	ap	ab	ba	pa
MN	NM	WN	MN	MW

Activity 3—Matching Words: In this example, the student circles the word on each line that is identical to the first word of that line. (Examples progress from simple to complex.)

big	car	big	was	ran
TOP	CAR	SAW	TOP	BAG
boy	big	bay	bag	boy
dog	god	dog	bog	dot

AUDITORY DISCRIMINATION

Children must be able to hear likenesses among and differences between sounds as they occur in spoken words. This ability or skill is known as *auditory discrimination*. A typical auditory discrimination test would ask children to recognize the fine differences between the phonemes used in English speech. For instance, children might be asked to say whether word pairs that are read to them sound exactly the same or different. Minimal word pairs that differ by a single phoneme in the beginning position (hot—cot), middle position (met—mit), and ending position (sad—sat) are used with word pairs that are identical (man—man) to measure this skill. One study attempting to predict first-grade reading success based on tests of visual discrimination, auditory discrimination, and auditory vocabulary (Spache, Andres, Curtis, Rowland, & Fields, 1965) found that measures of auditory discrimination were the best overall predictors. These results suggest that auditory discrimination is a significant factor in beginning reading.

It must be remembered that measures of auditory discrimination provide only partial data when differentiating between children who need training and children who do not. In using auditory discrimination data, the following considerations should be kept in mind: Poor performance may, in fact, reflect a hearing loss rather than a lack of auditory discrimination, and some speech sounds are often not mastered by the age of six or seven (Spache & Spache, 1986). These limitations, however, do not render auditory discrimination measures worthless. If the test results are used with limitations in mind and complemented by other pertinent data (i.e., teacher observations, classroom achievement, and medical information), auditory discrimination measures can provide valuable input regarding a child's readiness to use phonics in learning to read.

Auditory Awareness Exercises

Since oral language serves as the foundation on which reading skills are built, teachers should provide children with numerous experiences in both listening and speech. Activities similar to those listed here will allow children to "work" with language in a productive way.

Activity 1: Read to children daily. Nursery rhymes and rhyming books provide children with opportunities to experience similar sounds in a patterned manner.

Activity 2: Storybook reading provides opportunities for listening, but they should also provide children with meaningful opportunities for using oral language.

Activity 3: Have children identify the sounds heard in the classroom and around the school.

Activity 4: Have children close their eyes. Ask them to identify the sounds of snapping fingers, a pencil sharpener, tearing paper, chalkboard writing, and so on.

Activity 5: Play recordings of common sounds and have children identify them.

Activity 6: Have children play a game in which they have to identify sounds made by a child who imitates a sound from a specific place, such as a farm, airport, highway, zoo, and so on.

Auditory Discrimination Exercises

To provide more direct opportunities to improve auditory discrimination skills, you must have children work with the sounds of the English language, not simply sounds in general, as was done while building auditory awareness in the preceding examples. In addition, it is important for children to either hear someone else voicing the sounds or say the sounds themselves *out loud*. Too often, auditory discrimination activities require children to identify the sounds, as represented by pictures, silently as they make decisions about likenesses and differences rather than having them name the pictures out loud. Activities can be used to provide practice in beginning, middle, and ending sounds. The instructor should introduce beginning sounds first, followed by ending sounds and finally middle sounds. Although the following activities are designed to practice beginning-sound discrimination, they can be modified to include work on the endings and middles of words.

Activity 1: Read word pairs to the class (e.g., cot—hot; man—men; sin—pin). Ask if they begin with the same sound or a different sound. Always keep in mind that the language used to instruct must be understood by students. If, in this example, they do not know what "same" or "different" means, the strategy will have no value.

Activity 2: Have children listen to a series of words that begin with the same consonant sound. Ask children to identify other words that begin with the same sound.

Activity 3: Read a series of words to children (e.g., cat, come, cane, man), have the entire class repeat all the words together, and ask them to say the one that does not belong.

Activity 4: Provide beginning sounds for the children (e.g., /s/) and ask them to say words that begin with the same sounds.

Activity 5: Introduce children to rhyming words through the use of nursery rhymes and poetry.

CHAPTER 4: PRACTICE

1. Emergent literacy (is, is not) concerned with the earliest phases of literacy development, the period between birth and the time when children read and write conventionally. (Circle one.)

2. What is the relationship between oral language and reading achievement?

   _____

   _____

   _____

   _____

   _____

3. _____ _____ is the ability to recognize spoken words as a sequence of individual sounds.

4. Phoneme _____ is the ability to isolate all the sounds of a word.

5. Phoneme _____ is the process of recognizing isolated speech sounds and the ability to pronounce words for which they stand when combined.

6. The chapter identifies several skills that teachers can use to teach children to manipulate phonemes. What does research suggest about using a multiskilled approach to teach children to manipulate phonemes?

   _____

   _____

   _____

   _____

7. Numerous studies have shown that children who begin their schooling with knowledge of the ABCs are more likely to become better readers than children who lack this knowledge. Does it then follow that teaching children their ABCs will produce better readers? Why?

   _____

_____

_____

_____

_____

8. Why might a school cumulative file that contains information indicating that a child has successfully passed a vision test be misleading?

_____

_____

_____

_____

9. Having children practice visual discrimination for reading by using pictures and geometric shapes (is, is not) an effective procedure. (Circle one.)

10. What implications does the concept of emergent literacy hold for teachers of beginning reading?

_____

_____

_____

_____

_____

CUMULATIVE REVIEW: CHAPTERS 1 TO 4

1. A _____ is a part of the syllable that includes the vowel sound and any consonant sound(s) that come(s) after it.

2. A *single vowel sound* made up of a glide from one vowel to another in immediate sequence and pronounced in one syllable is called a _____.

3. A *phonogram* is the graphic representation of a _____.

4. Any syllable that ends with a vowel phoneme is called a(n) _____ syllable.

5. The sounds represented by *bl* in *blue* are called a _____
   _____.

6. A _____ is a soft vowel sound closely resembling the
   short sound of *u* that commonly occurs in unstressed syllables.

7. The _____ is a symbol placed over a vowel letter to show
   that it is pronounced as a short sound.

8. The phoneme /oi/ is an example of a _____.

9. (True–False) All digraphs are graphemes.

10. (True–False) All graphemes are digraphs.

11. If a child enters kindergarten reading at the third-grade level, do you
    believe that she should go through the phonics curriculum as set up by the
    district? Why?

    _____

    _____

    _____

12. Define the following phonic terms.

    Phoneme:

    _____

    _____

    _____

    Grapheme:

    _____

    _____

    _____

    Digraph:

    _____

    _____

    _____

    Onset:

    _____

    _____

    _____

13. (Phonics, Phonetics) is the method used to teach beginning reading.
    (Circle one.)

14. A closed syllable ends with a _____ _____.

15. A letter or combination of letters that represents a phoneme is called a _____.

16. (True–False) Implicit approaches to teaching phonics have proven more effective than explicit approaches.

17. A _____ is a unit of pronunciation that consists of a vowel alone or a vowel with one or more consonants.

18. An unstressed sound commonly occurring in unstressed syllables and very closely resembling the short *u* sound is a _____.

19. Provide a word that contains each of the following:

    Vowel digraph   _____

    Consonant digraph   _____

    Diphthong   _____

    Schwa   _____

    Blend   _____

    Open syllable   _____

    Closed syllable   _____

20. Underline any consonant or vowel digraph in the following words:

    stew   the   why   star   meet   shut   glove   good   sing   glut

21. Underline the digraphs in the following words that represent diphthongs:

    boy   could   owl   out   point   cow   boil   own   coin   town

22. Fill in the proper consonant phonemes for each of the underlined letter(s):

care	/ ____ /	song	/ ____ /
why	/ ____ /	phone	/ ____ /
measure	/ ____ /	whom	/ ____ /
sox	/ ____ / / ____ /	chemist	/ ____ /
quit	/ ____ / / ____ /	gym	/ ____ /

23. Fill in the proper vowel phonemes for each of the underlined letter(s):

dare	/ ____ /	order	/ ____ /
father	/ ____ /	star	/ ____ /
awful	/ ____ /	pearl	/ ____ /
rule	/ ____ /	good	/ ____ /
owl	/ ____ /	hurt	/ ____ /

24. How many phonemes are represented in the following words? Write each word using its phoneme pronunciation symbols:

plum	4	/p/ /l/ /ŭ/ /m/
off	____	_____
future	____	_____
naked	____	_____
true	____	_____
plume	____	_____
funny	____	_____
queen	____	_____
mix	____	_____
hare	____	_____

5 PHONIC GENERALIZATIONS

Much has been written about the utility of phonic generalizations over the past 35 years. Although some work in the area had been accomplished before 1960, an article by Clymer (1996) questioning the appropriateness of the many phonic generalizations taught at the time gave rise to several research projects designed to examine and extend what Clymer studied.

In essence, Clymer analyzed the instructor's manuals of four widely used primary-grade readers and identified 121 generalizations: 50 vowel generalizations, 15 consonant generalizations, 28 ending generalizations, and 28 syllabication generalizations. Of these, 45 generalizations were selected arbitrarily for further study (each had to be specific enough to be applied to individual words). A list of 2,600 words was developed by combining the words introduced in the four readers with the words from the Gates Reading Vocabulary for the Primary Grades. Using *Webster's New Collegiate Dictionary* as the pronunciation authority, each applicable word was checked against the appropriate generalization. From this check, a "percent of utility" was computed for each generalization. For instance, if 10 words could be applied to a generalization, five of which followed the generalization and five of which did not, the generalization would have a 50 percent utility.

At the beginning of the study, Clymer postulated that a 75 percent utility was indicative of a useful generalization. Only 18 of the 45 generalizations satisfied this utility criterion (Clymer, 1963, Table 1, pp. 50–53). The results of Clymer's study proved disturbing to him and others because they ran counter to what many instructors had been teaching for many years.

Clymer's research was followed by other studies on similar aspects of phonic generalizations. Bailey (1967) examined the 45 phonic generalizations studied previously by Clymer but extended the word list to include all words in the student textbooks from eight basal reading series, grades 1 through 6. She concluded that only six generalizations (Clymer's numbers 20, 22, 23, 28, 32, and 40 in Table 5.1) "were found to be simple to understand and apply, to be applicable to large numbers of words, and to have few exceptions" (p. 414). Emans (1967), using the same generalizations and procedures as Clymer, studied words beyond the primary level (grade 4) to determine the usefulness of phonic generalizations. He found that 16 of the 45 generalizations (Clymer's 5, 8, 16, 20, 22, 23, 24, 28, 30, 31, 32, 36, 38, 40, 41, and 45) met the criteria established by Clymer. Other studies by Burmeister (1968); Caldwell, Roth, and Turner (1978); Fuld (1968); Gates (1986); and Hillerich (1978) have addressed various aspects of phonic generalizations. Based on the results of those studies and an examination of current basal series, certain consonant and vowel generalizations stand out as having enough utility to be of value in phonics instruction.

Table 5.1 The Utility of 45 Phonic Generalizations

*Generalization	No. of words conforming	No. of exceptions	Percent of utility
1. When there are two vowels side by side, the long sound of the first one is heard, and the second is usually silent.	309 (bead)**	377 (chief) **	45
2. When a vowel is in the middle of a one-syllable word, the vowel is short.	408	249	62
middle letter	191 (dress)	84 (scold)	69
one of the middle two letters in a word of four letters	191 (rest)	135 (told)	59
one vowel within a word of more than four letters	26 (splash)	30 (flight)	46
3. If the only vowel letter is at the end of a word, the letter usually stands for a long sound.	23 (he)	8 (to)	74
4. When there are two vowels, one of which is final *e*, the first vowel is long, and the *e* is silent.	180 (bone)	108 (done)	63
*5. The *r* gives the preceding vowel a sound that is neither long nor short.	484 (horn)	134 (wire)	78
6. The first vowel is usually long and the second silent in the digraphs *ai*, *ea*, *oa*, and *ui*.	179	92	66
ai	43 (nail)	24 (said)	64
ea	101 (bead)	51 (head)	66
oa	34 (boat)	1 (cupboard)	97
ui	1 (suit)	16 (build)	6
7. In the phonogram *ie*, the *i* is silent, and the *e* has a long sound.	8 (field)	39 (friend)	17
*8. Words having double *e* usually have the long *e* sound.	85 (seem)	2 (been)	98
9. When words end with silent *e*, the preceding *a* or *i* is long.	164 (cake)	108 (have)	60
*10. In *ay* the *y* is silent and gives *a* its long sound.	36 (play)	10 (always)	78
11. When the letter *i* is followed by the letters *gh*, the *i* usually stands for its long sound, and the *gh* is silent.	22 (high)	9 (neighbor)	71

continued

Table 5.1 continued

*Generalization	No. of words conforming	No. of exceptions	Percent of utility
12. When *a* follows *w* in a word, it usually has the sound *a* as in *was*.	15 (watch)	32 (swam)	32
13. When *e* is followed by *w*, the vowel sound is the same as represented by *oo*.	9 (blew)	17 (sew)	35
14. The two letters *ow* make the long *o* sound.	50 (own)	35 (down)	59
15. *W* is sometimes a vowel and follows the vowel digraph rule.	50 (crow)	75 (threw)	40
*16. When *y* is the final letter in a word, it usually has a vowel sound.	169 (dry)	32 (tray)	84
17. When *y* is used as a vowel in words, it sometimes has the sound of long *i*.	29 (fly)	170 (funny)	15
18. The letter *a* has the same sound (ô) when followed by *l, w,* and *u*.	61 (all)	65 (canal)	48
19. When *a* is followed by *r* and final *e*, we expect to hear the sound heard in *care*.	9 (dare)	1 (are)	90
*20. When *c* and *h* are next to each other, they make only one sound.	103 (peach)	0	100
*21. *Ch* is usually pronounced as it is in *kitchen, catch,* and *chair,* not like *sh*.	99 (catch)	5 (machine)	95
*22. When *c* is followed by *e* or *i*, the sound of *s* is likely to be heard.	66 (cent)	3 (ocean)	96
*23. When the letter *c* is followed by *o* or *a*, the sound of *k* is likely to be heard.	143 (camp)	0	100
24. The letter *g* often has a sound similar to that of *j* in *jump* when it precedes the letter *i* or *e*.	49 (engine)	28 (give)	64
*25. When *ght* is seen in a word, *gh* is silent.	30 (fight)	0	100
26. When a word begins with *kn*, the *k* is silent.	10 (knife)	0	100
27. When a word begins with *wr*, the *w* is silent.	8 (write)	0	100
*28. When two of the same consonants are side by side, only one is heard.	334 (carry)	3 (suggest)	99

continued

Table 5.1 The Utility of 45 Phonic Generalizations—continued

*Generalization	No. of words conforming	No. of exceptions	Percent of utility
*29. When a word ends in *ck,* it has the same last sound as in *look.*	46 (brick)	0	100
*30. In most two-syllable words, the first syllable is accented.	828 (famous)	143 (polite)	85
*31. If *a, in, re, ex, de,* or *be* is the first syllable in a word, it is usually unaccented.	86 (belong)	13 (insect)	87
*32. In most two-syllable words that end in a consonant followed by *y,* the first syllable is accented, and the last is unaccented.	101 (baby)	4 (supply)	96
33. One vowel letter in an accented syllable has its short sound.	547 (city)	356 (lady)	61
34. When *y* or *ey* is seen in the last syllable that is not accented, the long sound of *e* is heard.	0	157 (baby)	0
35. When *ture* is the final syllable in a word, it is unaccented.	4 (picture)	0	100
36. When *tion* is the final syllable in a word, it is unaccented.	5 (station)	0	100
37. In many two- and three-syllable words, the final *e* lengthens the vowel in the last syllable.	52 (invite)	62 (gasoline)	46
38. If the first vowel sound in a word is followed by two consonants, the first syllable usually ends with the first of the two consonants.	404 (bullet)	159 (singer)	72
39. If the first vowel sound in a word is followed by a single consonant, that consonant usually begins the second syllable.	190 (over)	237 (oven)	44
*40. If the last syllable of a word ends in *le,* the consonant preceding the *le* usually begins the last syllable.	62 (tumble)	2 (buckle)	97

continued

Table 5.1—continued

*Generalization	No. of words conforming	No. of exceptions	Percent of utility
*41. When the first vowel element in a word is followed by *th, ch,* or *sh,* these symbols are not broken when the word is divided into syllables and may go with either the first or the second syllable.	30 (dishes)	0	100
42. In a word of more than one syllable, the letter *v* usually goes with the preceding vowel to form a syllable.	53 (cover)	20 (clover)	73
43. When a word has only one vowel letter, the vowel sound is likely to be short.	433 (hid)	322 (kind)	57
*44. When there is one *e* in a word that ends in a consonant, the *e* usually has a short sound.	85 (leg)	27 (blew)	76
*45. When the last syllable is the sound *r,* it is unaccented.	188 (butter)	9 (appear)	95

*Generalizations marked with an asterisk were found "useful" according to the criteria.
**Words in parentheses are examples—either of words that conform or of exceptions, depending on the column.
Source: Reprinted with permission of Ted Clymer and the International Reading Association.

CONSONANT GENERALIZATIONS

Consonant generalizations are more consistent than vowel generalizations. The following appear to offer the most instructional value:

1. *c* usually represents the "soft c" as in *cent* and *race* when followed by the letters *e, i,* or *y.* Otherwise, the *c* usually represents the "hard c" as in *coat* and *cot.*

2. *g* usually represents the "soft g" as in *gym* and *wage* when followed by the letters *e, i,* and *y.* Otherwise, the *g* usually represents the "hard g" as in *go* and *nag.*

When using these two generalizations above, children should be taught that there are exceptions. If, when attempting to identify a word, they find that the generalization does not appear to work, children should be encouraged to try the other sound before seeking help.

3. The consonant digraph *ch* is usually pronounced /ch/ as in *church* but may also represent the sounds of /k/ as in *chemical* or /sh/ as in *machine.*

4. When identical consonant letters are next to each other, only one is usually heard as in *letter*, *call*, and *cannon*.

5. Certain consonant letters represent more than one sound. (See also items 1 and 2.)

s		x	
smile	/s/	anxiety	/z/
is	/z/	mix	/k/ /s/
sure	/sh/	exit	/g/ /z/
pleasure	/zh/		

6. When a word ends in *ck*, it has the sound /k/ as in *book*.

7. When a word begins with *kn*, the *k* is silent as in *knit*.

8. When a word begins with *wr*, the *w* is silent as in *wrong*.

9. When a word begins with *gn*, the *g* is silent as in *gnat*.

VOWEL GENERALIZATIONS

Although the correspondence between vowel letters and sounds in English is less consistent than the correspondence between consonant letters and sounds, some consistency does exist and allows for the following vowel generalizations:

1. A single vowel letter in a syllable usually represents the short sound if it is not the final letter (cat, but, lot, met, mit).

2. A single vowel letter in a syllable usually represents the long sound if it is the final letter (he, hi, go, pa-per, ti-ger).

3. When two vowel letters in a syllable are separated by a consonant and one is a final *e*, the first usually records its long sound, and the *e* is silent (hope, late, cute).

4. When two successive vowel letters occur in a syllable and they are not any of the special digraphs (oi, oy, ow, ew, ou, oo, au), the first vowel letter is usually long and the second silent (especially ee—keep, ea—meat, ai—pain, ay—say, oa—load).

Because there are many exceptions to these generalizations, Spache and Spache (1986) recommend that children learn to use a systematic approach when meeting an unknown word. If the sound of the first letter or blend combined with context is not sufficient to "unlock" the word, a closer look at vowels is suggested. An application of appropriate vowel generalizations (see items 1 to 4) is used in the next attempt at correct pronunciation. If the vowel generalization fails, the other vowel sound should be attempted. Should these efforts fail, assistance from a dictionary or teacher would then be appropriate.

This systematic approach emphasizes that generalizations are only guidelines. When they do not work, other sounds should be attempted.

5. *ow* has two sounds, the /ō/ as in *own* and the /ou/ as in *cow.*

6. *oo* has two sounds, the /o͞o/ as in *food* and the /o͝o/ as in *foot.*

7. The *r* gives the vowel before it a sound that is neither long nor short.

8. The vowel digraphs *oi, oy, ou,* and *ow* blend into a single sound (diphthong) as in *boil, boy, out,* and *owl.*

9. *y* at the end of a word usually represents a vowel sound.

In teaching these generalizations, two approaches may be taken. One procedure would center on the teacher telling children about generalizations and having them apply those generalizations to specific words. This telling process is known as *deductive instruction.* For instance, a generalization like the following is taught first: "When there are two vowels side by side, the long sound of the first is heard, and the second is silent." Children are then asked to apply it to specific examples.

A second procedure would be described as *inductive instruction.* The inductive process begins with specifics and moves to generalizations about them. For instance, children might be asked to analyze the vowels in a group of words—boat, heat, rain, low—from which they will identify a common characteristic and ultimately develop a generalization to cover the pattern (in this example, first vowel long and second vowel silent).

Both approaches have their place in phonics instruction. For instance, inductive instruction provides children with opportunities for developing strategies of independent learning. On the other hand, deductive instruction has certain time advantages and can be used when efficient use of time becomes an important element in the teaching situation. In addition, not all children have success with the inductive approach. Consequently, a combination of the two processes can serve a valuable function in phonics instruction.

CHAPTER 5: PRACTICE

1. An analysis of Clymer's (1963) study reveals that _____ generalizations generally have a greater utility value than do _____ generalizations.

2. Circle the following nonsense words in which *c* would most likely represent the "soft c" sound:

   cint   cule   cymp   sluce

3. The consonant digraph *ch* usually represents the phoneme /_____/. However, it may also represent the phonemes /_____/ and /_____/.

4. When identical consonant letters are next to each other, (both, only one) (are, is) usually heard. (Circle one of each.)

5. (Deductive, Inductive) teaching begins with specifics and moves to generalizations. It is analytic in nature. (Circle one.)

6. Circle the following nonsense words in which *g* would most likely represent the "hard g" sound:

   giltion   gultion   buge   seg

7. When a word begins with *kn*, the *k* is _____.

8. When the _____ _____ *ck* ends a word, it represents the phoneme /_____/.

The following questions should be answered using the vowel generalization information presented earlier. Each question requires the vowel pronunciation contained in a nonsense word. Circle the correct answer.

9. The *e* in *slek* has the same sound as:
   a. *e* in *he.*
   b. *e* in *err.*
   c. *e* in *end.*
   d. *e* in *her.*
   e. None of the above.

10. The *a* in *swa* has the same sound as:
    a. *a* in *may.*
    b. *a* in *wand.*
    c. *a* in *add.*
    d. *a* in *art.*
    e. None of the above.

11. The *o* in *kote* has the same sound as:
    a. *o* in *cop.*
    b. *o* in *orange.*
    c. *o* in *go.*
    d. *o* in *out.*
    e. None of the above.

12. The *e* in *ceab* has the same sound as:
    a. *e* in *he.*
    b. *e* in *err.*
    c. *e* in *end.*
    d. *e* in *her.*
    e. None of the above.

13. The *o* in *woab* has the same sound as:
    a. *o* in *boy.*
    b. *o* in *go.*
    c. *o* in *out.*
    d. *o* in *cot.*
    e. None of the above.

14. The *u* in *knupe* has the same sound as:
    a. *u* in *up.*
    b. *u* in *run.*
    c. *u* in *hurt.*
    d. *u* in *use.*
    e. None of the above.

15. The *i* in *fif* has the same sound as:
    a. *i* in *high.*
    b. *i* in *girl.*
    c. *i* in *in.*
    d. *i* in *pine.*
    e. None of the above.

16. The *a* in *paic* has the same sound as:
    a. *a* in *art.*
    b. *a* in *name.*
    c. *a* in *map.*
    d. *a* in *swan.*
    e. None of the above.

17. A single vowel letter in a syllable usually represents the short sound if

    _____

    _____.

18. A single vowel letter in a syllable usually represents the long sound if

    _____

    _____.

19. When two vowel letters in a syllable are separated by a consonant and one is a final *e*, the first usually records its _____ sound, and the *e* is _____.

20. When two successive vowel letters occur in a syllable and they are not any of the special digraphs, the first usually records its _____ sound, and the second is _____.

CUMULATIVE REVIEW: CHAPTERS 1 TO 5

1. (True–False) It appears that a commitment to whole-word instruction is in direct opposition to using a phonics approach in any significant way.

2. The study of human speech sounds is called _____.

3. A _____ is the symbol used to represent a long vowel sound.

4. There is only one _____ phoneme in each syllable.

5. A phoneme is the _____ sound unit of a language that distinguishes one word from another.

6. The *oa* in *boat* is called a _____ .

7. _____ _____ is the ability to hear likenesses and differences among sounds as they occur in spoken words.

8. Readiness to read (is, is not) something that exists in an absolute sense. (Circle one.) Why?

   _____

   _____

   _____

   _____

   _____

9. In the words below, indicate the vowel phoneme represented by each underlined letter or pair of letters.

d<u>a</u>nce	/_____/	<u>aw</u>ful	/_____/
d<u>ou</u>ble	/_____/	<u>a</u>way	/_____/
p<u>u</u>t	/_____/	av<u>e</u>nge	/_____/
d<u>i</u>sk	/_____/	v<u>er</u>se	/_____/

10. In the words below, indicate the consonant phoneme represented by each underlined letter or pair of letters.

<u>g</u>in	/_____/	<u>wh</u>ere	/_____/
<u>g</u>oat	/_____/	<u>ph</u>onics	/_____/
<u>c</u>oat	/_____/	lu<u>x</u>	/_____/ / _____/
<u>w</u>ho	/_____/	<u>c</u>ent	/_____/

11. How many phonemes are represented in the following words? Write each word using its phoneme pronunciation symbols.

phone	_____	_____
out	_____	_____
knew	_____	_____
about	_____	_____
auto	_____	_____

could   _____   _____

toy   _____   _____

pearl   _____   _____

pudding   _____   _____

dare   _____   _____

12. Reading is a visual act that requires effective _____ vision.

13. _____ _____, the ability to hear sounds of varying pitch and loudness, is an important factor in beginning reading.

14. (True–False) Children who enter school with a knowledge of letter names are more likely to become better readers than children who lack this knowledge. Therefore, teaching children the letter names in kindergarten should eliminate many of our reading problems at the lower grade levels. Why?

_____

_____

_____

_____

_____

_____

_____

15. Research indicates that practicing visual discrimination for reading is best accomplished through what kind of activities?

_____

_____

_____

_____

_____

_____

6 | TEACHING CONSONANTS AND VOWELS

The most current basal reading series generally include a significant amount of phonics training at the lower levels. An examination of the phonics content of current basal series leads to several observations:

1. The scope and sequence of phonics in basal series vary widely, and research has not identified the best sequence in which decoding skills should be taught. Consequently, decisions about the order of instruction are often related to the words used in the basal series' stories.

2. Formal instruction begins with an emphasis on initial consonant sounds. This practice appears logical because (a) consonant sounds are more consistent in their spelling than are vowel sounds and so are less confusing to children, (b) written English has a left-to-right orientation whereby the initial position of words assumes the most significant position in word recognition, and (c) most of the words that children are initially asked to learn begin with consonant sounds.

3. Although initial emphasis is placed on consonants, there is an early introduction (readiness, preprimer, and primer texts) of some vowels that allows children to decode meaningful words from the very early stages of reading instruction and provides them with skills that allow some degree of independence.

4. Practically all phonics content is taught by the end of second grade. With the advent of the No Child Left Behind Act, however, there has been a significant initiative to introduce phonics content knowledge traditionally taught in first grade into the kindergarten curriculum. This has resulted in earlier presentation of all phonics material at each successive grade level. The developmental appropriateness of this material for some children remains to be evaluated. In most basal series, only a few of the most difficult or infrequent letter–sound combinations are taught as late as third grade.

5. Most basal reading series include word patterns or *phonograms* at the start of their reading programs.

As shown by these observations, not all consonant sounds are taught before vowels are introduced. Remember that some consonants rarely occur in words and need not be addressed in beginning reading. In addition, every word has at least one vowel letter.

CONSONANTS

A review of the consonant phonemes is in order here. As discussed in Chapter 3, there are 25 consonant phonemes, 18 of which are composed of single letters and seven of which are composed of two-letter combinations. Fill in a key word that contains the sound of each two-letter phoneme.

/b/	bat	/ch/	_____
/d/	did	/hw/	_____
/f/	fat	/ng/	_____
/g/	go	/sh/	_____
/h/	he	/th/	_____
/j/	jam	/TH/	_____
/k/	kid	/zh/	_____
/l/	let		
/m/	me		
/n/	no		
/p/	pan		
/r/	run		
/s/	sat		
/t/	ten		
/v/	very		
/w/	will		
/y/	yes		
/z/	zoo		

Up to this point in the text, an instructional emphasis has been placed on learning phonemes. In teaching phonics, however, one begins with letters or graphemes and teaches children to recognize the sounds that correspond to them. The difficulty of this task is proportionately related to the level of consistency existing between letters and sounds. Because consonants are far more consistent in their spelling–sound relationships than are vowels, they are less confusing to children. Still, various problems arise when teaching consonants.

Single Consonants

Of the 21 consonant letters, 17 are basically phonemically consistent when they occur by themselves and not in combination (digraphs) with other letters. These include the following:

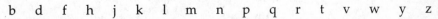

b   d   f   h   j   k   l   m   n   p   q   r   t   v   w   y   z

The four consonant letters that do not show a somewhat consistent one-to-one correspondence between letter and phoneme are *c, g, s,* and *x.* Each is discussed separately here.

The Letter C: C generally represents two phonemes, /k/ and /s/. (Remember, the letter *c* does not represent a phoneme identified by its own name.)

city	/s/	pact	/k/
coat	/k/	receive	/s/
rice	/s/	action	/k/

When the letter *c* represents /s/, it is commonly called the "soft c." When it represents /k/, it is commonly called the "hard c." Generally, the "hard c" is taught first because it occurs more frequently, especially as an initial letter in words.

The Letter G: G generally represents two phonemes, /g/ and /j/.

go	/g/	gull	/g/
gym	/j/	wage	/j/
agile	/j/	nag	/g/

When *g* represents /j/, it is commonly called the "soft g." When it represents /g/, it is commonly called the "hard g." Generally, the "hard g" is taught first for the same reasons that "hard c" is taught first: it occurs more frequently.

The Letter S: S generally represents two phonemes, /s/ and /z/, with /s/ being taught first.

smile	/s/	his	/z/
season	/z/	tops	/s/
is	/z/	test	/s/

The Letter X: X generally represents three phonemes: /z/, /k/ /s/, and /g/ /z/. (Remember that *x* does not represent a phoneme that is identified by its own name.)

sox	/k/ /s/	expect	/k/ /s/
exit	/g/ /z/ or /k/ /s/	mix	/k/ /s/
anxiety	/g/ /z/	xerox	/z/

Although the most common single letter–sound relationships have been previously discussed and should be adequate for phonics instruction, there are many exceptions to consider. Fortunately, they occur infrequently. Here is a sampling of some of these exceptions:

of	/v/
individual	/j/
pleasure	/zh/
sure	/sh/
cello	/ch/
think	/ng/

Consonant Blends (Clusters)

Consonant blends are sounds in a syllable represented by two or more letters that are blended together *without* losing their own identity. Although blends are actually separate sounds, they are dealt with together because they occur frequently in syllables. It should be noted that 15 of the 21 initial consonant blend combinations contain either an *r* or an *l*. The letters *l* and *r* belong to the same sound family. Many languages do not differentiate between the sounds of *l* and *r* and cannot hear the difference when English speakers use them in the initial position of words. The /l/ sound is often inserted into words as beginning readers attempt to decode them aloud. The intrusive /l/ sound helps the beginning reader define the vowel sound articulated after it. The /r/ sound is also intrusive but less often. The tendency to insert /l/ and /r/ diminishes as the reader gains proficiency.

Initial consonant blends frequently taught in current basal series include the following:

br	fr	tr	fl	sc	sn	sw
cr	gr	bl	gl	sl	sp	spr
dr	pr	cl	pl	sm	st	str

Final consonant blends frequently taught in current basal series include the following:

-ld	(cold)	-lk (walk)	-nd (pond)	-nk (drink)	-nt (want)
-mp	(lamp)	-sk (ask)	-st (last)	-ft (lift)	-lt (colt)

Consonant Digraphs

To review, consonant digraphs consist of two letters that stand for a single phoneme. Several letter combinations are classified as consonant digraphs. In teaching phonics, however, a limited number of these digraphs must be taught. Children should learn either that some letter combinations represent a new sound that is different from the sound represented by each letter separately or that one of the two letters is silent. Although basals vary in the consonant digraphs they teach, the following occur most frequently:

Initial Consonant Digraphs

ch	(chubby)	ph	(phone)	wh	(why)
gn	(gnat)	sh	(she)	wr	(wrong)
kn	(known)	th	(the)		

Ending Consonant Digraphs

-ch	(lunch)	-gh	(tough)	-ng	(sing)
-ck	(luck)	-ll	(call)	-ss	(class)
-ff	(off)	-mb	(lamb)	-th	(teeth)

Of these consonant digraphs, *th* and *ch* create the most confusion because they are inconsistent and frequently represent more than one sound.

The Consonant Digraph *Th:* *Th* can represent one of two phonemes, /th/ or /TH/. One is called a voiceless sound (/th/) because, when spoken, air is expelled and little vibration is created by the voice box or tongue. Try the following voiceless /th/ sounds:

thing	thigh	thank	thumb
bath	ether	cloth	teeth

The other sound associated with the consonant digraph *th* is called a voiced sound (/TH/) because, when spoken, little air is expelled and a definite vibration is created in the voice box and by the tongue. Try the following voiced /TH/ sounds:

then	clothe	this	these
thy	their	bathe	either

When teaching the sounds associated with *th*, it is not necessary to burden children with the terms *voiceless* and *voiced*. Simply pointing out to children the fact that *th* can represent one of two sounds as heard in designated key words will suffice.

The Consonant Digraph *Ch:* *Ch* usually represents the phoneme /ch/, as in *church*. Less frequently, *ch* represents the phoneme /k/, as in *chemical*, and the phoneme /sh/, as in *machine*.

VOWELS

Because of the inconsistent nature of the sounds that vowel letters represent, teaching vowel sounds is the most difficult task in phonics instruction. Because of this inconsistency, one must be careful to avoid any vowel instruction that will confuse rather than assist children in attacking unknown words. An examination of the phonics content of current basal series leads to several observations:

1. The scope and sequence of vowel instruction varies widely. Research has not identified the best sequence in which vowels should be taught.

2. Although formal instruction places initial emphasis on consonant sounds, vowels are introduced early. Vowel instruction is begun at either the readiness and preprimer text levels or the primer text level.

3. The greater part of vowel instruction up to first grade is devoted to short vowel sounds and long vowel sounds as represented by certain vowel digraphs (*ai, ay, ea, ee*) or words having the spelling pattern, vowel-consonant-e (i.e., *hope, take*).

4. Increased attention is being given to teaching vowel sounds within particular rimes as represented by phonograms. This approach takes advantage of

the fact that vowel sounds are far more stable within particular rimes than they are in isolation.

5. The schwa sound is often introduced at approximately the second- or third-grade level. It is generally taught as the initial sound of a two-syllable word beginning with the letter *a*, such as *about*.

6. Instruction in some of the most difficult vowel digraphs and diphthongs is delayed until third grade.

A review of the 19 vowel phonemes follows:

/ā/	age	/ē/	ease	/ī/	ice	/ō/	old	/ū/	use
/ă/	an	/ĕ/	end	/ĭ/	in	/ŏ/	odd	/ŭ/	up
/oi/	oil (diphthong)			/ou/	out (diphthong)		
/o͞o/	too	/o͝o/	good	/ə/	about		
/â/	dare	/û/	her	/ä/	father	/ô/	off

As mentioned earlier in this chapter, when teaching phonics, one begins with letters or graphemes and teaches children to recognize the sounds that correspond to them. Because vowels are not consistent in their spellings, this becomes a formidable task.

Short–Long Vowel Sounds

Short vowel sounds are usually introduced in three-letter words with a spelling pattern of consonant-vowel-consonant (CVC). This is expanded to include words that follow the spelling patterns VC and CVCC. Several techniques can be used for formal instruction of short vowels. Two examples follow:

1. Using phonograms to build word families. For instance, using the phonogram *ig*, one could develop the following word family: big, dig, pig, fig, wig.

2. Changing the vowel sound in known words to make new words: big, bag; dig, dog; wig, wag.

In contrast to short vowels, long vowels are usually introduced in words with a spelling pattern of VCe, as in *whale*. This is expanded to include certain vowel digraphs (*oa* in *boat*) and single-syllable words ending in a vowel (*o* in *go*).

Children are often taught or led to discover generalizations that will assist them in identifying short and long vowel sounds. The following examples are from basal series and illustrate varied approaches.

Silver Burdett Ginn (1993): "Say these words, elongating the vowel sound as you say each one: *man, pet, pin, nod, tub*. Point out that these words all have short vowel sounds. Say these words: *mane, Pete, pine, rode, tube*. Explain that these words all have long vowel sounds. Write each set of words on the chalkboard and have children compare both sets. Lead them to see that short vowel words have a consonant-vowel-consonant pattern and long vowel words have a consonant-vowel-consonant-*e* pattern" (p. T71).

Houghton Mifflin (1997c): "Have children read the first two sentences on page 10 with you. Ask them to listen for the vowel sounds in *no* and *mop*. Write the words on the chalkboard. Ask these questions:

What vowel sound do you hear in *mop*? (short *o*)

Do you hear the same vowel sound in *no*? (*no*)

Remind children that the vowel sound in *no* is the long *o* sound. Label the CV pattern in *no*. You may also want to have children contrast these words: not-no; got-go" (p. T69).

Vowel Digraphs

Vowel digraphs are two-vowel letters that stand for a single sound or phoneme. Several letter combinations are classified as vowel digraphs. In teaching phonics, however, only a limited number of these digraphs must be taught because many vowel digraphs are not consistent enough in their spelling–sound relationships to justify teaching them.

An analysis of current basal series reveals that most include instruction for the following vowel digraphs:

Vowel Digraphs	Phonemes
ee, ea	/ē/
ai, ay	/ā/
oa, ow	/ō/
oo	/o͞o/
oo	/o͝o/
ou, ow	/ou/ (diphthong)
oi, oy	/oi/ (diphthong)
au, aw	/ô/

In teaching vowel digraphs, basals tend to emphasize the most common sound represented by specific digraph combinations. These basals also point out that some vowel digraphs (*oi, oy, ou, ow, oo*) are special cases and represent sounds that are neither long nor short.

R-Controlled Vowels

Children are taught that when a vowel is followed by the consonant letter *r*, the vowel sound is neither short nor long:

Read aloud the sentence on page 18 and point out the word *shark*. Explain that when a vowel is followed by an *r*, the vowel sound is neither long nor short, and that the letters *ar* often stand for the vowel sound heard in *shark*.

Ask children to look on page 19 and find three other words in which *ar* stands for the sound heard in *shark* (*are, far, apart*).

Next, explain that the sound for *o* followed by *r* is neither long nor short. Ask a volunteer to read page 20. Point to *for* and explain that the letters *or* often stand for the vowel sound in *for* (Houghton Mifflin, 1997a, p. T257).

Schwa

The schwa sound is introduced at approximately the second- or third-grade level and is often taught in conjunction with syllabication and/or dictionary use. Although the schwa sound may be represented by any of the vowel letters, little attention is given to the teaching of the schwa sound.

A schwa is a short, unstressed vowel that often occurs in unaccented sylla-bles. Therefore, children would have to divide words into proper syllables, iden-tify which syllables are unaccented, and finally determine which vowels were schwas. Obviously, this systematic approach is beyond the capabilities of young children. Little instructional attention, therefore, is given to teaching children how to decode the schwa sound in a technical, systematic manner. Fortunately, since the schwa sound is a soft vowel sound that is similar to the short *u* sound, children often come close enough to the sound to render a correct pronunciation in their decoding attempts.

Teaching Vowels Through Phonograms

Wylie and Durrell (1970) conducted a study showing that the following 37 phonograms can be combined with various consonant letters to generate approximately 500 primary words:

-ack	-ail	-ain	-ake	-ale	-ame	-an
-ank	-ap	-ash	-at	-ate	-aw	-ay
-eat	-ell	-est	-ice	-ick	-ide	-ight
-ill	-in	-ine	-ing	-ink	-ip	-it
-ock	-oke	-op	-ore	-ot	-uck	-ug
-ump	-unk					

Wylie and Durrell (1970) found that children learned the vowel sounds con-tained in phonograms more easily compared to learning these sounds through individual letter–sound correspondences or phonic generalizations.

CHAPTER 6:   PRACTICE

1. The inconsistent spelling of (consonant sounds, vowel sounds) is a basic problem of phonics. (Circle one.)

2. There are _____ vowel phonemes in the English language.

3. The _____ sound is a short, unstressed vowel that often occurs in unaccented syllables.

4. There (is, is not) a best sequence in which vowels should be taught. (Circle one.)

5. Of the 21 single consonant letters, four are phonemically inconsistent and represent more than one sound. Alphabetically list these four consonant letters, indicate the phonemes they can represent, and write out a key word for each.

Letter	*Phonemes*	*Words*
_____	/___/ , /___/	_____ , _____
_____	/___/ , /___/	_____ , _____
_____	/___/ , /___/	_____ , _____
_____	/___/	_____
	/___/ /___/	_____
	/___/ /___/	_____

6. The "soft c" is represented by the phoneme /___/.

   The "hard c" is represented by the phoneme /___/.

   The "soft g" is represented by the phoneme /___/.

   The "hard g" is represented by the phoneme /___/.

7. (Consonant digraphs, Consonant blends) are sounds in a syllable represented by two or more letters that are combined without losing their individual identity. (Circle one.)

8. Can you discriminate between consonant digraphs and consonant blends? Write "D" after letter combinations that represent digraphs and "B" after letter combinations that represent blends.

br _____	pl _____	-ck _____	-sk _____
ch _____	sh _____	-nk _____	-ld _____
cl _____	wh _____	-mp _____	-ng _____
kn _____	pr _____	-mb _____	-st _____
th _____	gr _____	-nt _____	-nd _____

9. Short and long vowels are often introduced in words with certain spelling patterns. Are the following patterns short or long?

   CVC   _____

   CV   _____

   VCe   _____

   VC   _____

10. What is the advantage of teaching vowel sounds within phonograms as compared to teaching them in isolation?

_____

_____

_____

_____

_____

CUMULATIVE REVIEW: CHAPTERS 1 TO 6

1. Phonics (appears, does not appear) to be the panacea for most reading ills. (Circle one.)

2. Phonics instruction should be completed by the end of _____ grade for most children.

3. Define the following terms:

Phonics:

_____

_____

_____

Phoneme:

_____

_____

_____

Open Syllable:

_____

_____

_____

Macron:

_____

_____

_____

Consonant:

_____

_____

_____

Digraph:

_____

_____

_____

Syllable:

_____

_____

_____

4. Underline any consonant or vowel digraph contained in the following words:

out   book   blunt   stun   that

dare   song   chat   knob   clip

5. A _____ of two letters is called a digraph.

6. Fill in the proper consonant phoneme for each of the following underlined letter(s):

cage   /__/   queen   /__/ /__/

who   /__/   sox   /__/ /__/

knew   /__/   cell   /__/

measure   /__/   critique   /__/

7. Fill in the proper vowel phoneme for each of the underlined letter(s):

air   /__/   toe   /__/

senator   /__/   call   /__/

otter   /__/   house   /__/

turn   /__/   good   /__/

8. How many phonemes are represented in the following words? Write each word using its phoneme pronunciation symbols.

red   _____   _____

coat   _____   _____

wheel   _____   _____

quit   _____   _____

who   _____   _____

when   _____   _____

fly   _____   _____

curse   _____   _____

dialect   _____   _____

9. What is emergent literacy, and how does it affect learning to read once children enter school?

_____

_____

_____

_____

_____

_____

_____

10. Studies have shown that children who begin their schooling knowing the ABCs are more likely to become better readers than children who lack this knowledge. Of what importance is this fact for teachers of beginning reading?

_____

_____

_____

_____

_____

11. Write out the vowel generalization that the words below follow:

coat:

_____

_____

_____

hope:

_____

_____

_____

she:

_____

_____

_____

but:

_____

_____

_____

12. Why is it more effective to teach vowel *generalizations* than vowel *rules*?

_____

_____

_____

_____

_____

_____

_____

_____

_____

_____

7 | SYLLABICATION AND ACCENTING

At first glance, especially for those who are competent readers, the process of syllabication appears to be a somewhat simple task. On closer examination, however, it reveals itself to be a rather complex process that many children find quite difficult. Why, then, should the process be taught to children? The answer lies in the fact that unless some systematic procedure is used when attempting to decode multisyllabic words, the process essentially becomes one of trial and error. By providing children with strategies for syllabication, the amount of trial and error needed to decode unknown words is reduced significantly; even though a certain amount of trial and error will remain, it becomes less random and more directed.

A *syllable* is a basic unit of pronunciation consisting of a vowel alone or a vowel with one or more consonants. There is one—and only one—sounded vowel (phoneme) in each syllable. Phonic generalizations pertain to syllables, not to words, which means that syllables, not words, are initially decoded. For this reason, the vowel generalizations presented in Chapter 5 were stated in terms of syllables.

As children begin to work with an increasing number of unknown polysyllabic words, they first must be able to syllabicate them correctly before applying vowel generalizations. Since they cannot divide unknown words by sound, they must rely on certain spelling patterns and/or generalizations to assist them in this task.

Before attempting to teach children syllabication strategies or generalizations, the prerequisite skills of hearing and recognizing syllables in words, understanding letter–sound relationships, and knowing the useful phonic generalizations must be learned by them. It is not unusual, then, for the topic of syllabication to be introduced as late as the second or third grade.

Children are commonly introduced to syllabication by getting them to hear syllables in words they already know. The activity of clapping each syllable as they say words is often used at this introductory stage of instruction. Although it is appropriate to have children practice syllabication with known words at the onset of instruction when the concept is introduced, it is inappropriate to have children continue to practice their syllabication skills only on known words. To be effective, reinforcement and practice must be done using unknown words. Therefore, the practice items offered in this chapter consist mostly of nonsense words. These will encourage the mature readers of this text to experience and use the strategies and generalizations that their students will need to use when they attempt to decode unknown multisyllabic words. Syllabication generalizations that should assist children in their attempts to decode multisyllabic words include the following.

1. Every syllable contains one—and only one—vowel sound. This concept is best developed by helping children recognize syllables in words they already know. This task is accomplished through providing children with varied opportunities to hear and recognize syllables in spoken words. Eventually, children should be able to pronounce familiar words in syllabic form. Once children understand the concept of syllabication and know letter–sound relationships and appropriate phonic generalizations, attention turns to an analysis of word structure and the spelling patterns of words.

2. Most affixes (prefixes and suffixes) are syllables. Children are taught to look first for common word parts (prefixes and suffixes) that they have learned previously. Some of the most common prefixes and suffixes follow:

Prefix

dis-	in-	non-	sub-
em-	inter-	over-	un-
en-	ir-	pre-	
im-	mis-	re-	

Suffix

-able	-est	-ly	-y
-al	-ful	-ment	
-en	-ing	-ness	
-er	-less	-ion (-tion)	

Often, more specific generalizations related to affixes are taught as follows:

a. *-ture* and *-tion* are syllables (e.g., pic-ture, ma-ture, cap-tion, lo-tion).

b. The inflected *-ed* adds a syllable when affixed to a verb ending in *-d* or *-t*. Otherwise, it does not add a syllable (e.g., need-ed, root-ed, stayed, asked).

3. In a compound word, the syllabic division usually comes between the words of which it is composed. Syllabicate divided compound words according to other generalizations.

4. When a word ends in *-le* preceded by a consonant, the consonant plus *-le* make up a syllable (e.g., mid-dle, ar-ti-cle). It also usually contains a schwa sound.

5. When two vowel letters appear together, they usually represent one sound and should be viewed as a single grapheme when syllabicating. Burmeister (1966) examined the validity of this generalization using randomly selected words from the *Teacher's Word Book of 30,000 Words* (Thorndike & Lorge, 1944) and found that 84.5 percent of the time it proved true. In addition, one-third of the exceptions occurred when the vowel pair *ia* appeared in words such as *giant*.

6. Letters representing consonant digraphs, especially *th, ch,* and *sh,* and consonant blends are treated as single consonants and are not separated when words are broken into syllables.

7. Although double consonant letters are generally separated when words are broken into syllables via writing, the sound will be represented in only one syllable as follows:

common	com-mon	kŏm-ən
latter	lat-ter	lăt-ər
connote	con-note	kə-nōt

Once the specific generalizations previously described are addressed, the following generalizations are applied:

8. When two consonant letters are between two vowel letters, a syllabic division often occurs between the consonants. A current basal series expresses this generalization as follows: "Most VCCV words are divided into syllables between the consonants" (Houghton Mifflin, 1997b, p. 323E).

9. When there is one consonant letter between two vowel letters, the consonant often goes with the next syllable. This generalization has less consistency than does number 8 above (see Table 5.1, numbers 38 and 39). For this reason, basals usually present options as follows: "Most VCV words with the short-vowel pattern in the first syllable are divided after the consonant because the consonant is part of the short-vowel pattern. Most VCV words with a long-vowel sound or a *schwa* sound in the first syllable are divided before the consonant" (Houghton Mifflin, 1997b, p. 323E). Thus, students are told when they attempt to figure out an unfamiliar word syllable by syllable that they "might have to make several attempts, trying different pronunciations and stressing different syllables, before coming up with a word that sounds familiar" (Houghton Mifflin, 1997b, p. 323E).

In terms of accenting, two generalizations should suffice:

1. In two-syllable words, the accent is usually on the first syllable.
2. Prefixes and suffixes are generally not accented.

As you teach children generalizations that apply to syllabication and accenting, it is important to teach the concept that these provide a starting point in their attempts to decode words. If students' efforts yield words that do not make sense or are unknown, alternative efforts should be attempted. Teachers should no longer attempt to teach these generalizations as though they were *rules* that produce results without failure.

CHAPTER 7:   PRACTICE

1. In a two-syllable word, the accent is usually on the _____ syllable.

2. Every syllable contains one—and only one—_____ sound.

3. Most affixes (are, are not) syllables. (Circle one.)

4. The inflected -*ed* adds a syllable when affixed to a verb that ends with either the letter _____ or _____.

5. When a word ends in -*le* preceded by a consonant, the consonant plus -*le* make up a syllable. When -*le* is preceded by a vowel, the *e* is usually _____.

6. Letters representing consonant digraphs, especially *th, ch,* and *sh,* and consonant blends are treated as single consonants and (are, are not) separated when words are broken into syllables. (Circle one.)

7. When two vowel letters appear together, they usually represent _____ sound.

8. When two consonant letters are between two vowel letters, a syllabic division often occurs _____ _____ _____.

9. In writing, double consonant letters are usually broken up into separate syllables. In speech, how is the pronunciation of double consonants handled?

   _____

   _____

   _____

   _____

   _____

   _____

10. Identify the syllabic divisions (as occurs in writing) in the following vowel–consonant letter patterns, nonsense words, or words. There are no consonant digraphs in the first seven letter patterns. In the space provided, indicate which generalization(s) you used to accomplish this task.

    Vowel-Consonant Letter Patterns

    VCV   _____
    VCCV   _____
    VCVC   _____
    CVCCV   _____
    CCVCCVC   _____
    CCVCVC   _____
    VCe   _____ (Special VCV when final letter is *e*)

    Real Words

    amass   _____   _____
    aphis   _____   _____
    beldam   _____   _____

retable   _____   _____
bolide   _____   _____
cupule   _____   _____
foxed   _____   _____
furbelow   _____   _____
judicature   _____   _____

Nonsense Words

preanthema   _____   _____
unboted   _____   _____
emakle   _____   _____
epeture   _____   _____
grapeet   _____   _____
resired   _____   _____
ecad   _____   _____
antole   _____   _____
scrnt   _____   _____
mashot   _____   _____
haulm   _____   _____
subtonen   _____   _____

CUMULATIVE REVIEW: CHAPTERS 1 TO 7

1. There (are, are not) significant research data that show the importance of phonics in beginning reading instruction. (Circle one.)

2. The latest research suggests the advantages of systematic synthetic phonics instruction (outweigh, do not outweigh) the disadvantages. (Circle one.)

3. Circle each of the following terms that refers to a letter or letters:

   phoneme vowel grapheme rime diphthong digraph consonant onset phonogram

4. Besides *a, e, i, o,* and *u,* what other two letters sometimes represent vowels? _____ and _____.

5. Circle each of the following words that contains a closed syllable:

   gone   so   sew   dove   tire   dough

6. Underline any consonant digraph contained in the following words:

   blade   ring   that   steel   shucks   chain   tree

7. Underline any vowel digraphs contained in the following words:

   few   good   feet   dove   oil   soup   letter

8. Phoneme _____ is the ability to isolate all sounds of a word.

9. The phonogram is the graphic representation of a _____.

10. The phonemes /oi/ and /ou/ are examples of a _____.

11. There are _____ phonemes in the English language, _____ consonant sounds, and _____ vowel sounds.

12. Circle the words that contain the /o͞o/ sound:

    too   good   room   shoes   stood   look

13. The letters ___ , ___ , and ___ do not represent phonemes that are identified by their own names.

14. A single vowel letter in a syllable usually represents the short sound if

    _____

    _____.

15. When two successive vowel letters occur in a syllable and they are not any of the special digraphs, the first usually records its _____ sound and the second is _____.

16. Fill in the proper vowel or consonant phoneme for each underlined letter(s).

    pl<u>ai</u>d   /___/   plea<u>s</u>ure   /___/
    m<u>a</u>re   /___/   lo<u>ng</u>   /___/
    sk<u>y</u>   /___/   basi<u>c</u>   /___/
    t<u>oy</u>   /___/   <u>gh</u>ost   /___/

17. When a cumulative file contains information indicating a child has successfully passed a vision test, why might this information be misleading?

    _____

    _____

    _____

    _____

    _____

18. What relationship appears to exist between oral language and reading achievement?

    _____

    _____

    _____

    _____

_____

_____

_____

_____

19. What is the difference between phoneme segmentation and phoneme blending? Provide an example of each approach.

_____

_____

_____

_____

_____

_____

_____

20. Workbooks and other paper-and-pencil activities require students to learn or practice phonics silently. Is this an effective approach? Why?

_____

_____

_____

_____

_____

_____

_____

21. What is the difference between a synthetic (explicit) approach to teaching phonics and an analytical (implicit) approach?

_____

_____

_____

_____

_____

_____

22. Formal instruction in phonics usually begins with an emphasis on initial
    _____ sounds. Why?

    _____

    _____

    _____

    _____

    _____

    _____

23. Identify a phonogram and indicate how to instructionally develop a word
    family.

    _____

    _____

    _____

    _____

    _____

    _____

24. How does the ability to syllabicate words assist children in their attempts
    to pronounce unknown words?

    _____

    _____

    _____

    _____

    _____

    _____

25. Define the following terms.

    Phonetics:

    _____

    _____

    _____

Grapheme:

_____

_____

_____

Vowels:

_____

_____

_____

Diphthong:

_____

_____

_____

Consonant Blend:

_____

_____

_____

Rime:

_____

_____

_____

Schwa:

_____

_____

_____

8 | DIAGNOSTIC TEACHING

The goal of every teacher should be to provide an environment in which children are allowed the opportunity to grow toward their full potential. This learning environment can be accomplished only if teachers are able to identify the individual strengths and weaknesses of students and can develop instructional strategies that take advantage of this knowledge. In essence, it requires every classroom teacher to participate in diagnostic teaching.

To assume this diagnostic role effectively, teachers need to become aware of the general principles of diagnosis as well as the elements of diagnosis related to specific content areas. Discussion of both the general principles of diagnosis and the specific procedures for diagnosing phonics follow.

GENERAL PRINCIPLES OF DIAGNOSIS

General diagnostic principles include the following:

1. Diagnosis should be viewed as a daily occurrence. Diagnosis is too often treated as a special event that takes place only once or twice a year. In reality, teachers need to observe and evaluate children on a continuing basis because children's needs and/or skills can change drastically over a short period.

2. Decisions about children should be based on diagnostic information collected from various sources. Instructional decisions about children should never be made on the basis of a single test or observation, and these decisions must be based on facts, not opinions. Generally, the more diverse the data that teachers collect, the more useful the information.

3. The identification of patterns of errors should be emphasized when analyzing diagnostic information. If a type of error occurs in a pattern, greater confidence can be placed on the interpretation that the error is truly a problem for the child. When decisions are based on isolated errors, unneeded instruction and practice often follow.

4. Work on only one or two reading weaknesses at a time. Often, when diagnosing children who exhibit problems in reading, several weaknesses will be identified. If attempts are made to remediate all these weaknesses at once, it generally overwhelms the children and further frustrates their efforts to improve. Narrow the skills to be taught to the one or two that appear to create the most difficulty and remediate these before continuing with others that are less debilitating.

5. Diagnosis for its own sake is not acceptable; it must lead to specific instructional action. Teachers must avoid becoming so enamored of the diagnostic process that they lose sight of the ultimate objective of diagnosis—the identification and remediation of weaknesses or disabilities. An exception to this occurs when pre-service teachers or clinical practicum students are learning to administer informal reading inventories or other diagnostic measures. In this case, some amount of practice and expertise using the instrument is required.

The procedures for evaluating phonic skills are varied and include both informal and formal diagnosis. The following is a sample of procedures teachers can use and items they can construct to assist them in diagnosing students' phonic skills.

PROCEDURES FOR DIAGNOSING PHONIC SKILLS

Observation

During a typical school day, teachers have many opportunities to observe and collect pertinent information about the reading proficiencies of students. To take advantage of these opportunities, teachers need to devise written systems that allow them to record their observations over time. These, in turn, can be analyzed later to identify weaknesses or patterns of error. One frequently required form of informal assessment is the running record. Running records are teacher-produced reading samples that are coded while an individual reader reads aloud. They are designed for efficient classroom application and generally take less time than traditional reading inventories. It is typical for a teacher to conduct multiple running records for each child in her class during the school year. These observations can also be used to verify or question results gathered through more formalized data collections.

There is no best way to collect and categorize observational data. This process can be as simple as developing a file for each child and recording observations by date as they occur, similar to the system used by medical doctors. Or more specific observational documents can be constructed by teachers to identify the exact phonic skills to be observed. For example, if one of the skills a teacher decides to analyze is the ability to pronounce initial consonants correctly in single-syllable words, the teacher can simply construct a sheet with the consonant letters listed on it and mark them off as children pronounce each consonant. Teachers can observe and/or develop recording sheets related to phonic elements such as single-letter consonant sounds, double-letter consonant sounds, consonant blends, long vowels, short vowels, r-controlled vowels, diphthongs, vowel combinations (especially *ee, ea, ai, ay, oa*), double *o*, knowledge of vowel and consonant generalizations, phoneme segmentation, and phoneme blending.

Informal Reading Inventory

The informal reading inventory (IRI) is a more formal procedure for observing, recording, and analyzing children's reading proficiencies. Generally, these inventories attempt to measure, through the oral reading of a set of graded word lists and paragraphs, both the word recognition and the comprehension skills of those taking the test. As the examinee reads the word lists and paragraphs for the word recognition part of the inventory, all errors are recorded on a sheet that is later used to analyze and categorize the types of errors that the examinee made (similar to the teacher's written comments mentioned in the previous section, "Observation").

The IRI has certain limitations that teachers should recognize. It can be administered to only one person at a time and requires a significant amount of time to administer and analyze. For these reasons, many reading authorities feel that it is impractical to recommend that the IRI be administered to every child in a class. Rather, it might best be administered to those who are having significant problems in reading and about whom teachers feel they need more information. Another limitation that must be recognized is the fact that data from an IRI are but one sample of behavior that has been gathered at a specific point in time. The data may or may not be representative of the child's real skills. Therefore, even if an IRI is given, the data should be tested by comparing the results to data gathered through teacher observations and other evaluative procedures.

Several standardized tests fall under the category of informal reading inventories. Some that are common in the field include the following:

Analytical Reading Inventory, Sixth Edition, by Mary Lynn Woods and Alden J. Moe. (1999). Upper Saddle River, NJ: Prentice Hall.

Basic Reading Inventory, Fifth Edition, by Jerry L. Johns. (1991). Dubuque, IA: Kendall/Hunt.

Classroom Reading Inventory, Seventh Edition, by Nicholas J. Silvaroli. (1994). Dubuque, IA: Brown & Benchmark.

Phonemic Awareness

A high correlation exists between the ability to recognize spoken words as a sequence of individual sounds and reading achievement. We have seen that explicit instruction can increase the phonemic awareness of children. To assist in determining the level of phonemic awareness in children, the following assessment items can be used.

Assessment 1:   Isolation of beginning sounds. Ask the child what the first sounds of selected words are.

"What is the first sound of *dog*?"

Assessment 2:   Deletion of initial sound. Read a word and ask the child to say it without the first sound.

"Say the word *cat*. Say *cat* without the /k/."

To begin, it is probably better to use words that will remain words when the first letter is eliminated.

Assessment 3:   Segmentation of phonemes. Ask the child to say aloud the separate sounds of a word that is read.

"What are the two sounds in the word *go*?"

Assessment 4:   Blending of phonemes. Slowly read the individual sounds of a word and ask the child to say what the word is.

"What word am I saying? /d/ /ô/ /g/."

Assessment 5:   Phoneme manipulation. Read a word and ask the child to replace the initial sound with another. Have the child say the new word.

"In the word *fan*, the first sound is an /f/. If you replace the /f/ with an /m/, how would you say the new word?"

Letter Names

As discussed earlier in Chapter 4, knowledge of letter names is not a prerequisite for learning to read. Although knowledge of letter names on entering school appears to be a predictor of later reading success, the relationship between knowing letter names and reading achievement is not one of cause and effect. Based on a review of the research related to this issue, however, Groff (1984) states,

> At present, the following conclusion seems tenable: Letter name teaching is appropriate if done concurrently with instruction in phonics. Those who contend that the time of letter name teaching is unimportant probably are wrong.
> Since letter name knowledge and phonics knowledge are highly correlated, it makes sense to view them as functionally related areas of information. Thus, simultaneous teaching appears to be the best way to exploit their potential for helping children to learn to read. (p. 387)

Thus, it seems desirable at the beginning stages of reading instruction to assess children's knowledge of letter names. This information can be gleaned through assessments similar to those listed next.

Assessment 1:   Develop flash cards for each letter of the alphabet, starting with lowercase. (Once lowercase letters are known, this exercise can be expanded to include uppercase letters.) In random order, present each card to the examinee and ask the student to name the letter. Record the examinee's responses on a scoring sheet. These data can be used to determine the appropriate letter name instruction for each child.

Assessment 2:   Have the examinee write the letters of the alphabet as they are dictated in a random order. Analyze the results to determine which letters the examinee knows. Since the goal is letter name knowledge, either lower- or uppercase responses are correct. Responses that show the reverse (i.e., mirror image) form of a letter should also be considered correct.

Consonant Sounds

Several types of items can be used to determine if children understand the relationship between consonants and the letters that represent them. Most of the following examples offer ways of measuring recognition of the initial letter or letters of words (a) because of the essential role that this position plays in decoding words and (b) because this is the position that is addressed first in instruction. However, the same kinds of assessments can be constructed for the endings of words as well.

Assessment 1: Letter to sound—single-consonant letters. Using flash cards of 19 single consonant letters (*q* and *x* do not have to be addressed at the beginning level), ask the child to say the sound represented by each. Record the child's responses.

Assessment 2: Letter to sound—single-consonant letters/pictures. Show the child a consonant letter followed by three pictures that name something. Ask the child to identify the picture whose name begins with the same sound as represented by the consonant letter. As examiner, name each picture slowly. Record the child's responses. The same 19 single-consonant letters as indicated in assessment 1 should be evaluated.

> m   [pictures of a]   (ball)   (moon)   (toy)

Assessment 3: Sound to letter—single-consonant letters. Provide the child with a score sheet that has four consonant letters after each item. For each, say a word and tell the child to circle the consonant letter that represents the first sound of the word.

> toy   s   t   m   p

Assessment 4: Sound to letter—single-consonant letters. Have the child write the beginning letter of each word that you read. Vary words to include all 19 consonant letters mentioned in assessment 1.

Assessment 5: Letter to sound—consonant digraphs. Using flash cards of consonant digraphs (*th, ch, sh, wh*), ask the child to say the sound represented by each letter pair. Record the child's responses.

Assessment 6: Letter to sound—consonant digraphs/pictures. Show the child a consonant digraph followed by three pictures that name something. Ask the child to identify the picture whose name begins with the same sound as represented by the two letters. As examiner, name each picture slowly. Record the child's responses. The same four consonant digraphs as indicated in assessment 3 should be evaluated.

> sh   [pictures of a]   (ship)   (church)   (sun)

Assessment 7:   Sound to letters—consonant digraphs. Provide the child with a score sheet that has four consonant digraphs after each item. For each, say a word and tell the child to circle the consonant digraph that represents the first sound of the word.

chin   sh   th   ch   wh

Assessment 8:   Sound to letters—consonant digraphs. Have the child write the first two letters of each word that you read. Vary the words so that they begin with *sh, th, ch,* and *wh.*

Assessment 9:   Consonant letters representing blends. Using flash cards of letters representing several blends, ask the child to say the sound represented by each. Record the child's responses.

Assessment 10:   Consonant letters representing blends/pictures. Show the child letters representing consonant blends followed by three pictures that name something. Ask the child to identify the picture whose name begins with the same sounds as represented by the consonant letters. As examiner, name each picture slowly. Record the child's responses.

tr   [pictures of a]   (top)   (train)   (thumb)

Assessment 11:   Consonant letters representing blends—sound to letters. Provide the child with a score sheet that has letters representing four consonant blends after each item. For each, say a word and tell the child to circle the letters that represent the first sounds of the word.

blue   bl   st   br   fl

Assessment 12:   Consonant letters representing blends—sound to letters. Have the child write the first two letters of each word that you read. Vary the words to include several beginning blends.

Assessment 13:   Consonant letters representing blends—phonograms. Construct words combining common phonograms (i.e., *an, ill, ig*) with letters representing blends. After reading and emphasizing the rime (the sound of a phonogram) part of the word family, ask the child to read the words of the family. Record the child's responses. Children may need the examiner to model this behavior for a couple of families.

an   bran   stan   blan   clan

Vowel Sounds

The following assessments measure children's knowledge about vowels.

Assessment 1:   Long and short vowels. Display flash cards of the five vowel letters (*a, e, i, o, u*) and ask the child to identify verbally the long sound and the short sound of each. Record the child's responses.

Assessment 2:   Short vowels. Read sets of three words, each containing the same medial vowel sound (short), and have the examinee write or verbally indicate what vowel sound the words contain. Vary sets to include all short vowel sounds.

pin	bit	him

Assessment 3:   Short vowels. Develop sets of five words (some will be nonsense words*) that vary only by a medial vowel. Have the child read each word list. Record the child's responses.

mat	pan	sap
met	pen	sep
mit	pin	sip
mot	pon	sop
mut	pun	sup

Assessment 4:   Long vowels. Read sets of three words, each containing the same medial vowel sound (long), and have the examinee write or indicate verbally what vowel sound the words contain. Vary sets to include all long vowel sounds.

site	night	hive

Assessment 5:   Long vowels (vowel–consonant–final *e* pattern). Develop sets of five words following the VCe pattern (some will be nonsense words), each with a different initial vowel letter. Have the child read each word list. Record the child's responses.

cake	pete	sime	rote	mute
gate	scene	mite	home	fuse
sate	pese	like	hoke	cube

Assessment 6:   Short vowels (CVC) and long vowels (CVe). Develop a list of real-word and nonsense-word pairs that vary by a final *e*. Have the child read the word list and ask why she pronounced the words that way. Record the child's responses.

rote	rot
mit	mite
make	mak
set	sete
tune	tun

---

*When evaluating phonic skills with items that require the examinee to go from graphs to sounds, it is important to use words that are not part of the child's sight vocabulary. Therefore, this assessment and several that follow include nonsense words as a guard against obtaining misleading information.

Assessment 7: Vowel digraphs. Develop a list of real words and nonsense words that contain the vowel digraphs (*ee, ea, ai, ay, oa*). Have the child read the word list. Record the child's responses.

keep	say
teap	mait
seat	seet
tay	boat
pain	soan

Assessment 8: Special digraphs. Develop a list of real words and nonsense words that contain special vowel digraphs (*oi, oy, ou, ow, oo, au*). Have the child read the word list. Record the child's responses.

soil	mou
koo	boy
out	poit
poy	cow
too	sook
dow	maul
good	paut

Assessment 9: r-controlled vowels. Develop a list of real words and nonsense words that contain r-controlled vowels. Have the child read the word list. Record the child's responses.

car	sert
purm	dare
turn	lar
sare	firm
term	kirn

CONCLUSION

It is not the intention of this chapter to suggest that teachers should construct instruments that contain all the assessment items discussed in the chapter. The teacher is in the best position to determine what diagnostic information may be needed. Therefore, the representative assessment items included in the text should be considered as resource data from which teachers can pick and choose to assist in developing their own teacher-made assessment instruments. Finally, it should be restated at this point that the skills data that are collected from teacher-made and/or standardized tests should be verified or brought into question by observing and analyzing children as they attempt to use these skills in the act of reading.

CHAPTER 8: PRACTICE

1. Define what you believe diagnostic teaching to be.

   _____

   _____

   _____

   _____

   _____

   _____

   _____

   _____

   _____

2. To be effective, why is it necessary for teachers to become involved in diagnostic teaching?

   _____

   _____

   _____

   _____

   _____

   _____

   _____

3. Phonemic awareness, the ability to recognize spoken words as a sequence of individual sounds, shows a high correlation with reading achievement. Describe the following phoneme activities:

   a. Phoneme Blending

   _____

   _____

   _____

   _____

b. Phoneme Segmentation

_____

_____

_____

_____

4. Discuss each of the five general principles of diagnosis as listed below:

a. Diagnosis should be viewed as a daily occurrence.

_____

_____

_____

_____

b. Decisions about children should be based on diagnostic information collected from various sources.

_____

_____

_____

_____

c. The identification of patterns of errors should be emphasized when analyzing diagnostic information.

_____

_____

_____

_____

d. Work on only one or two reading weaknesses at a time.

_____

_____

_____

_____

e. Diagnosis for its own sake is not acceptable.

_____

_____

_____

_____

CUMULATIVE REVIEW: CHAPTERS 1 TO 8

1. Define the following vocabulary before attempting the post-test in Chapter 9. If you encounter significant problems, go back to the text and review before continuing.

   a. Phonics:

   _____

   _____

   _____

   b. Phonetics:

   _____

   _____

   _____

   c. Phoneme:

   _____

   _____

   _____

   d. Phonemic Awareness:

   _____

   _____

   _____

   e. Consonant:

   _____

   _____

   _____

f. Consonant Blend:

_____

_____

_____

g. Vowel:

_____

_____

_____

h. Diphthong:

_____

_____

_____

i. R-Controlled Vowel:

_____

_____

_____

j. Schwa Sound:

_____

_____

_____

k. Grapheme:

_____

_____

_____

l. Digraph:

_____

_____

_____

m. Onset:

_____

_____

_____

n. Rime:

_____

_____

_____

o. Phonogram:

_____

_____

_____

p. Syllable:

_____

_____

_____

q. Closed Syllable:

_____

_____

_____

r. Open Syllable:

_____

_____

_____

s. Breve:

_____

_____

_____

t. Circumflex:

_____

_____

_____

u. Macron:

_____

_____

_____

v. Umlaut:

_____

_____

_____

FILL IN THE BLANKS

1. _____ is a method in which basic phonetics, the study of human speech sounds, is used to teach beginning reading.

2. A(n) _____ is placed over a vowel letter to show that it is pronounced as a long sound.

3. A(n) _____ is two letters that stand for a single phoneme.

4. A(n) _____ syllable ends with a consonant phoneme.

5. Sounds in a syllable represented by two or more letters that do not lose their own identity when blended together are known as _____ _____ .

6. A(n) _____ is the smallest sound unit of a language that distinguishes one word from another.

7. A single vowel sound made of a blend of two vowel sounds in immediate sequence and pronounced in one syllable is known as a(n) _____ .

8. _____, made up of a letter or combination of letters, represent phonemes.

9. A(n) _____ is a letter sequence comprised of a vowel grapheme and an ending consonant grapheme(s).

10. _____ are units of pronunciation consisting of a vowel alone or a vowel with one or more consonants.

TRUE–FALSE

_____ 11. The irregularity of consonant sounds is a basic problem of phonics.

_____ 12. The schwa sound usually has a consistent spelling.

_____ 13. Phonics is *not* the most important skill required for effective reading.

_____ 14. Almost any letter may, at some time, be silent.

_____ 15. A grapheme must be composed of one and only one letter.

_____ 16. Each syllable must contain only one vowel sound.

_____ 17. In attacking multisyllabic words, children must syllabicate before applying vowel generalizations.

_____ 18. There are over 200 ways to spell the 44 phonemes.

_____ 19. By the time the average child enters school, his or her auditory discrimination skills are fully developed.

_____ 20. The history of phonics shows that a phonics approach to teaching reading has been looked on favorably by most reading authorities over the past 50 years.

MULTIPLE CHOICE

_____ 21. Which of the following is a sound?
   a. consonant
   b. grapheme
   c. digraph
   d. None of the above

_____ 22. Which of the following words contains an open syllable?
   a. dove
   b. dog
   c. threw
   d. fire

_____ 23. Which of the following words contains a consonant digraph?
   a. blue
   b. string
   c. fly
   d. home

_____ 24. Which of the following words contains letters that represent a diphthong?
   a. show
   b. seat
   c. through
   d. out

_____ 25. How many phonemes are represented by the word _knight_?
   a. 2
   b. 3
   c. 4
   d. 5

_____ 26. How many phonemes are represented by the word _through_?
   a. 1
   b. 2

    c. 3

    d. 4

_____ 27. Which of the following pairs contains the same vowel phoneme?

    a. took—room

    b. grew—too

    c. food—wool

    d. None of the above

_____ 28. Which of the following letters do *not* represent phonemes that are identified by their own name?

    a. c and s

    b. b and d

    c. y and x

    d. x and c

_____ 29. Which of the following consonant letters are most phonemically inconsistent in representing more than one sound?

    a. b and d

    b. c and g

    c. r and t

    d. m and p

_____ 30. Which of the following letter pairs represents a consonant blend?

    a. th

    b. fl

    c. zh

    d. wh

_____ 31. Which of the following nonsense words would most likely represent the "soft c" sound?

    a. cumb

    b. cimp

    c. cople

    d. calobe

_____ 32. Which of the following nonsense words would most likely represent the "hard g" sound?

    a. gilture

    b. weg

    c. gymp

    d. tuge

_____ 33. Which of the following consonant letters affects the vowel that precedes it?

    a. s

    b. t

    c. r

    d. None of the above

_____ 34. Which of the following words does *not* contain a consonant blend?
   a. street
   b. chin
   c. brown
   d. fly

_____ 35. Which of the following words contains a closed syllable?
   a. grow
   b. why
   c. boy
   d. rote

Circle the item in each list that does not belong. Explain your reason for each choice.

36. phoneme   digraph   diphthong   vowel

_____

37. th   tw   ch   ng   wh

_____

38. got   home   low   boy   high

_____

39. boy   pout   ounce   toil   double

_____

40. cuple   capon   cepp   cobat

_____

How many phonemes are represented in the following words? Write each word using its phoneme pronunciation symbols.

41. blue   _____   _____

42. herd   _____   _____

43. toxic   _____   _____

44. should   _____   _____

45. who   _____   _____

46. air   _____   _____

47. quit   _____   _____

48. antique   _____   _____

49. said   _____   _____

50. school   _____   _____

The following questions should be answered by using the vowel generalizations that are often taught in elementary schools. Each question requires the vowel pronunciation contained in a nonsense word.

_____ 51. The *i* in *dif* has the same sound as:

    a. girl.

    b. in.

    c. sight.

    d. None of the above.

_____ 52. The *u* in *smupe* has the same sound as:

    a. hurt.

    b. pup.

    c. use.

    d. None of the above.

_____ 53. The *a* in *kna* has the same sound as:

    a. mart.

    b. ate.

    c. map.

    d. None of the above.

_____ 54. The *e* in *reab* has the same sound as:

    a. bee.

    b. err.

    c. send.

    d. None of the above.

_____ 55. The *i* in *lirp* has the same sound as:

    a. bin.

    b. high.

    c. whirl.

    d. None of the above.

_____ 56. The *u* in *nupp* has the same sound as:

    a. hurt.

    b. cup.

    c. prude.

    d. None of the above.

_____ 57. The first *e* in *zeet* has the same sound as:

    a. me.

    b. err.

    c. send.

    d. None of the above.

_____ 58. The *u* in *tue* has the same sound as:

    a. cup.

    b. hurt.

    c. use.

    d. None of the above.

Indicate where the syllabic divisions occur in the following vowel-consonant letter patterns, nonsense words, or real words. Knowledge of syllabication generalizations is essential. There are no consonant digraphs in questions 59 to 62 (C = consonant letter, V = vowel letter).

_____ 59. CVCVCC
   a. CV-CV-CC
   b. CVC-VCC
   c. CV-CVCC
   d. CVCV-CC

_____ 60. CVCCVC
   a. CV-CCVC
   b. CVCC-VC
   c. CVC-CVC
   d. CV-CC-VC

_____ 61. VCCVC
   a. VC-CVC
   b. V-CCVC
   c. VCC-VC
   d. VCCVC

_____ 62. CCVCVCC
   a. CCVC-VCC
   b. CCV-C-VCC
   c. CC-VC-VCC
   d. CCV-CVCC

_____ 63. ralagasins
   a. ra-la-ga-sins
   b. ral-a-ga-sins
   c. ral-ag-a-sins
   d. ra-la-gas-ins

_____ 64. soctaluca
   a. soc-ta-lu-ca
   b. soc-tal-u-ca
   c. soct-al-u-ca
   d. soct-a-lu-ca

_____ 65. plukle
   a. pluk-le
   b. plukle
   c. pl-u-kle
   d. plu-kle

_____ 66. exanphema
   a. exan-phe-ma
   b. ex-an-phe-ma
   c. ex-an-phem-a
   d. e-xan-phe-ma

_____ 67. megmer

    a. me-gmer
    b. meg-mer
    c. megm-er
    d. megmer

Reading programs often introduce long and short vowel sounds based on spelling patterns. In the following patterns (V = vowel letter; C = consonant letter), indicate which vowel sound you would expect the pattern to represent (L = long sound; S = short sound).

_____ 68. VC

_____ 69. VCe (_e_ = final _e_ in word)

_____ 70. CVCC

_____ 71. CV

APPENDIX
Answer Key

CHAPTER 1: PRACTICE

1. is not
2. second
3. contextual, structural
4. letters, sounds
5. synthetic
6. Analytic
7. Answers will vary.
8. In learning phonics, children must have the opportunity to *see, hear,* and *say* the components they are being asked to learn. Initial instruction and practice in phonics should concentrate, therefore, on oral activities.
9. The purpose of phonics is to assist children in systematically decoding words that are unknown to them by teaching them the relationships that exist between letters and speech sounds. Phonics for the sake of phonics should never be the goal of instruction.
10. Systematic synthetic phonics instruction has a positive effect on reading skills. The advantages of asking students to articulate phonemes in isolation outweigh the disadvantages.

CHAPTER 2: PHONICS PRETEST

1. b
2. f
3. h
4. e
5. a
6. d
7. j
8. i
9. c

10. g
11. True
12. False
13. False
14. True
15. True
16. False
17. True
18. False
19. False
20. False
21. b
22. c
23. b
24. d
25. c
26. c
27. b
28. d
29. b
30. b
31. a
32. b
33. c
34. b
35. b
36. *th* is a consonant digraph, and the others are letters that represent consonant blends.
37. *st* represents a consonant blend, while the others are consonant digraphs.
38. *s* is the only letter that does not, at some time, represent a vowel sound.
39. *low* is the only word that does not contain letters representing the diphthong sound.
40. *gym* is the only word that contains a "soft g."
41. b
42. c
43. c
44. b

45. b
46. d
47. b
48. c
49. b
50. c
51. a
52. d
53. b
54. a
55. d
56. b
57. b
58. S
59. L
60. S
61. L

CHAPTER 2: PRACTICE

Answers will vary.

CUMULATIVE REVIEW: CHAPTERS 1 AND 2

1. contextual analysis, structural analysis
2. is not
3. are
4. outweigh
5. has not
6. synthetic
7. As children build larger sight vocabularies, they appear to rely less on phonics in many cases and more on the power of analogy: comparing unknown words to words that are known. Once children build this storehouse of words and progress beyond the beginning levels of reading, such elements as background knowledge, vocabulary, and general ability to reason become significantly more important in comprehending text.

8. *Explicit* or synthetic phonics emphasizes the learning of individual sounds, often in isolation, and follows with instruction that teaches children how to blend these individual sounds to form words (a part-to-whole approach). *Implicit* or analytic phonics, on the other hand, begins with whole words and identifies individual sounds as parts of those words. Efforts are made to avoid pronouncing letter sounds in isolation (a whole-to-part approach).

9. The whole language philosophy is certainly compatible with the teaching of phonics. Because of its emphasis on a whole-to-part approach, it would tend to emphasize implicit or analytic phonics.

10. Although the reader may pronounce an unknown word correctly, if it is not part of her speaking-listening vocabulary, she would have no way of knowing whether she was correct.

CHAPTER 3: PRACTICE

1. phoneme, vowel, rime, diphthong, consonant
2. a, e, i, o, u, y, w
3. go, dew, through
4. digraph
5. bri<u>ng</u>, <u>the</u>, <u>sh</u>ut, <u>ch</u>ill
6. <u>dew</u>, l<u>oo</u>k, s<u>ou</u>p, b<u>oy</u>, b<u>ea</u>t
7. diphthong, /ou/
8. sound
9. macron
10. breve
11. digraph
12. closed
13. digraph
14. phonetics
15. 44, 25, 19
16. inconsistent
17. vowel sounds
18. too—shoes
19. a. coil /oi/
    b. out /ou/
    d. owl /ou/
20. *c, q, x*

21. /s/ /zh/
 /k/ /f/
 /n/ /j/
 /sh/ /h/
 /ng/ /g/
 /hw/ /k/

22. /ā/ /û/
 /ī/ /ă/
 /oi/ /ou/
 /ū/ /ŏo/
 /ŏ/ /ĕ/
 /ōo/ /ŭ/

23. 2, /s/ /ō/
 3, /s/ /ĭ/ /ng/
 3, /b/ /l/ /ōo/
 4, /g/ /ō/ /s/ /t/
 3, /sh/ /ĭ/ /p/
 3, /ō/ /l/ /d/
 2, /b/ /oi/
 4, /b/ /û/ /r/ /d/
 3, /b/ /ō/ /th/
 4, /b/ /ŏ/ /k/ /s/
 4, /s/ /ĕ/ /n/ /t/
 3, /k/ /ō/ /m/
 2, /k/ /ou/
 2, /l/ /ō/

24. *Vowel:* sounds represented by *a, e, i, o, u,* and sometimes *y* and *w.*

 Grapheme: a letter or combination of letters that represnts a phoneme.

 Phoneme: the smallest sound unit of a language that distinguishes one word from another.

 Consonant: sounds represented by any letter of the English alphabet except *a, e, i, o,* and *u.*

 Syllable: a unit of pronunciation that consists of a vowel alone or a vowel with one or more consonants. There is only one vowel phoneme in each syllable.

 Macron: the orthographic symbol (ˉ) placed over a vowel letter to show that it is pronounced as a long sound.

Open syllable: any syllable that ends with a vowel phoneme.

Breve: the orthographic symbol (˘) placed over a vowel letter to show that it is pronounced as a short sound.

Digraph: two letters that stand for a single phoneme.

Rime: the part of a syllable that includes the vowel sound and any consonant sound(s) following it.

CUMULATIVE REVIEW: CHAPTERS 1 TO 3

1. are
2. has
3. <u>bl</u>end, <u>str</u>eet
4. Answers will vary. (Example: few)
5. Synthetic
6. Analytic
7. Phonics helps only if the unknown word is part of the reader's speaking-listening vocabulary.
8. whole-word. *Pneumonia* does not follow many phonic generalizations, especially vowel generalizations. Consequently, efforts spent with a whole-word emphasis would most likely produce better results.
9. A *digraph* is two *letters* that stand for a single phoneme, while a *diphthong* is a single vowel *sound* made up of a glide from one vowel to another. For example, in the word *oil,* the letters *oi* form the digraph, while the sound /oi/ is the diphthong.
10. A consonant digraph is two *letters* that stand for a single sound. A consonant blend is a combination of *sounds* in a syllable represented by two or more letters that are blended together without losing their own identities.
11. A phonogram is a letter sequence comprised of a vowel grapheme and an ending consonant grapheme(s). A rime is the sound a phonogram represents.
12. The *r* renders the vowel neither long nor short. (Examples: st<u>ar</u>, d<u>ar</u>e, h<u>er</u>, f<u>or</u>)
13. Learning letter–sound associations enables children to apply this knowledge in the process of decoding unknown words.

CHAPTER 4: PRACTICE

1. is
2. Oral language serves as an essential foundation on which reading instruction can and should be built.
3. Phonemic awareness

4. segmentation

5. blending

6. In instruction the focus on one or two skills produces greater transfer than a multiskilled approach. Phoneme segmentation and blending are basic and belong in beginning instructional programs.

7. There is no cause-and-effect relationship between knowledge of ABCs and effective reading. This knowledge is simply indicative of a host of factors that are often conducive to learning to read.

8. Reading is a visual act that requires effective near-point (close) vision. Yet the types of tests often administered to children at the beginning stages of schooling simply measure far-point (distant) vision.

9. is not

10. Teachers need to realize that the wide range of experiences that children have had with language before formal schooling begins should be used in assisting them to learn to read. Children's understanding about print awareness, concepts of print, sense of story, oral language, and writing will have a significant bearing on their ultimate success in reading achievement.

CUMULATIVE REVIEW: CHAPTERS 1 TO 4

1. rime

2. diphthong

3. rime

4. open

5. consonant blend

6. schwa

7. breve

8. diphthong

9. True

10. False

11. No. Phonics should be viewed as a means to an end.

12. *Phoneme:* the smallest unit of a language that distinguishes one word from another.

    Grapheme: a letter or combination of letters that represents a phoneme.

    Digraph: two letters that stand for a single phoneme.

    Onset: the consonant sound(s) of a syllable that come(s) before the vowel sound.

13. Phonics

14. consonant phoneme

15. grapheme
16. False
17. syllable
18. schwa
19. Answers will vary.
20. st<u>ew</u>, <u>the</u>, <u>why</u>, star, m<u>ee</u>t, <u>sh</u>ut, glove, g<u>oo</u>d, sin<u>g</u>, glut
21. b<u>oy</u>, could, <u>owl</u>, <u>out</u>, p<u>oi</u>nt, c<u>ow</u>, b<u>oi</u>l, own, c<u>oi</u>n, t<u>ow</u>n
22. Fill in the proper consonant phoneme for each of the underlined letter(s).

    /k/   /ng/
    /hw/   /f/
    /zh/   /h/
    /k/ /s/   /k/
    /k/ /w/   /j/

23. Fill in the proper vowel phonemes for each of the underlined letter(s).

    /â/   /ô/
    /ä/   /ä/
    /ô/   /û/
    /o͞o/   /o͝o/
    /ou/   /û/

24. 2, /ô/ /f/
    5, /f/ /ū/ /ch/ /û/ /r/
    5, /n/ /ā/ /k/ /ĭ/ /d/
    3, /t/ /r/ /o͞o/
    4, /p/ /l/ /o͞o/ /m/
    4, /f/ /ŭ/ /n/ /ē/
    4, /k/ /w/ /ē/ /n/
    4, /m/ /ĭ/ /k/ /s/
    3, /h/ /â/ /r/

CHAPTER 5: PRACTICE

1. consonant, vowel
2. cint, cymp, sluce
3. /ch/, /k/, /sh/
4. only one, is
5. Inductive
6. gultion, seg

7. silent
8. consonant digraph, /k/
9. c
10. a
11. c
12. a
13. b
14. d
15. c
16. b
17. it is not the final letter.
18. it is the final letter.
19. long, silent
20. long, silent

CUMULATIVE REVIEW: CHAPTERS 1 TO 5

1. False
2. phonetics
3. macron
4. vowel
5. smallest
6. digraph
7. Auditory discrimination
8. is not. It is quite possible that a child will be ready to learn under one set of instructional conditions and not be ready to learn under another.
9. /ă/   /ô/
   /ŭ/   /ə/
   /ŏo/   /ĕ/
   /ĭ/   /û/
10. /j/   /hw/
    /g/   /f/
    /k/   /k/ /s/
    /h/   /s/
11. 3, /f/ /ō/ /n/
    2, /ou/ /t/
    2, /n/ /o͞o/

4, /ə/ /b/ /ou/ /t/
3, /ô/ /t/ /ō/
3, /k/ /ŏo/ /d/
2, /t/ /oi/
4, /p/ /û/ /r/ /l/
5, /p/ /ŏo/ /d/ /ĭ/ /ng/
3, /d/ /â/ /r/

12. near-point
13. Auditory acuity
14. False. The relationship is not one of cause and effect. Knowledge of letter names does not cause one to become a better reader.
15. Visual discrimination must be done with letters and/or words. Practice with geometric figures and pictures does not transfer to the type of visual discrimination needed for reading.

CHAPTER 6: PRACTICE

1. vowel sounds
2. 19
3. schwa
4. is not
5. (Answer for words will vary.)

c	/s/, /k/
g	/g/, /j/
s	/s/, /z/
x	/z/
	/k/ /s/
	/g/ /z/

6. /s/
   /k/
   /j/
   /g/
7. consonant blends
8.

B	B	D	B
D	D	B	B
B	D	B	D
D	B	D	B
D	B	B	B

9. CVC   short
    CV   long
    Vce   long
    VC   short

10. Vowel sounds are far more stable within particular phonograms than they are in isolation.

CUMULATIVE REVIEW: CHAPTERS 1 TO 6

1. does not appear

2. second

3. *Phonics:* A method in which basic phonetics is used to teach reading.

    Phoneme: The smallest sound unit of a language that distinguishes one word from another.

    Open syllable: Any syllable that ends with a vowel phoneme.

    Macron: The symbol (¯) placed over a vowel letter to show it is pronounced as a long sound.

    Consonant: A sound represented by any letter of the English alphabet except *a, e, i, o, u.*

    Digraph: Two letters that stand for a single phoneme (sound).

    Syllable: A unit of pronunciation consisting of a vowel alone or a vowel with one or more consonants. There is only one vowel phoneme in each syllable.

4. <u>ou</u>t, b<u>oo</u>k, <u>th</u>at
    so<u>ng</u>, <u>ch</u>at, <u>kn</u>ob

5. grapheme

6. /k/   /k/ /w/
    /h/   /k/ /s/
    silent   /s/
    /zh/   /k/

7. /â/   /ō/
    /ə/   /ô/
    /ŏ/   /ou/
    /û/   /ŏŏ/

8. 3, /r/ /ĕ/ /d/
    3, /k/ /ō/ /t/
    3, /hw/ /ē/ /l/
    4, /k/ /w/ /ĭ/ /t/
    2, /h/ /ōō/

3, /hw/ /ĕ/ /n/

3, /f/ /l/ /ī/

4, /k/ /û/ /r/ /s/

7, /d/ /ī/ /ə/ /l/ /ĕ/ /k/ /t/

9. "Emergent literacy is concerned with the earliest phases of literacy development, the period between birth and the time when children read and write conventionally. The term *emergent literacy* signals a belief that, in a literate society, young children—even one- and two-year olds— are in the process of becoming literate" (Sulzby & Teale, 1991, p. 728). Thus, if young children have had little opportunity to experiment with reading and writing before they enter school, it can have a significant negative impact on their achievement.

10. Answers will vary. However, the fact that the relationship is not one of cause and effect should be included in the answer. Knowledge of letter names does not cause one to become a better reader.

11. *Coat:* When two successive vowel letters occur in a syllable and they are not any of the special digraphs (oi, oy, ow, ou, oo, au), the first is usually long and the second is silent (especially ee—keep, ea—meat, ai—pain, ay—say, oa—load).

    Hope: When two vowel letters in a syllable are separated by a consonant and one is a final *e*, the first usually records its long sound, and the *e* is silent.

    She: A single vowel letter in a syllable usually represents the long sound if it is the final letter.

    But: A single vowel letter in a syllable usually represents the short sound if it is not the final letter.

12. The term *generalizations* better represents the fact that there are exceptions to the letter–sound associations we teach children.

CHAPTER 7: PRACTICE

1. first

2. vowel

3. are

4. d, t

5. silent

6. are not

7. one

8. between the consonants.

9. Although double consonant letters are generally separated when words are broken into syllables in writing, the sound will be represented in only one syllable.

10. *Vowel-Consonant Letter Patterns*

V-CV	#9
VC-CV	#8
V-CVC	#9
CVC-CV	#8
CCVC-CVC	#8
CCV-CVC	#9
VCe	No division, as final e̲ is silent

Real Words

a-mass	#9
a-phis	#6, #9
bel-dam	#8
re-ta-ble	#2, #4
bo-lide	#9
cu-pule	#9
foxed	#2b
fur-be-low	#5, #8, #9
ju-di-ca-ture	#2a, #9

Nonsense Words

pre-an-the-ma	#2, #6, #8, #9
un-bot-ed	#2, #2b
e-ma-kle	#4, #9
e-pe-ture	#2a, #9
gra-peet	#5, #9
re-sired	#2, #2b
e-cad	#9
an-tole	#8
scrnt	no vowel letter, no vowel sound, no word
ma-shot	#6, #9
haulm	#5
sub-ton-en	#2

CUMULATIVE REVIEW: CHAPTERS 1 TO 7

1. are
2. outweigh
3. grapheme, digraph, phonogram

4. *y, w*

5. gone, dove, tire

6. ri<u>ng</u>, <u>th</u>at, <u>sh</u>ucks, <u>ch</u>ain

7. <u>few</u>, <u>goo</u>d, <u>fee</u>t, <u>oi</u>l, s<u>ou</u>p

8. segmentation

9. rime

10. diphthong

11. 44, 25, 19

12. too, room, shoes

13. *c, q, x*

14. it is not the last letter

15. long, silent

16. /ă/   /zh/

    /â/   /ng/

    /ī/   /k/

    /oi/   /g/

17. Reading is a visual act that requires effective near-point vision. Yet the types of tests often administered to children at the beginning stages of school measure only far-point vision.

18. Research has shown that a positive relationship exists between oral language and reading achievement. Oral language appears to serve as an essential foundation on which reading instruction can and should be built.

19. Segmentation is the process of isolating all the sounds of a word, while blending is the process of recognizing isolated speech sounds and the ability to pronounce the word for which they stand. (Examples will vary.)

20. No. To be effective, phonics instruction must be oral in nature. Children need to hear and speak the language to get the full benefit of instruction.

21. The synthetic approach generally emphasizes the learning of individual sounds, often in isolation, and follows with instruction that teaches children how to blend these individual sounds to form words (a part-to-whole approach). The analytic approach, on the other hand, begins with whole words and identifies individual sounds as part of those words. Efforts are made to avoid pronouncing letter sounds in isolation (a whole-to-part approach).

22. consonant. Consonants are more consistent in their spelling than are vowel sounds. Written English has a left-to-right orientation whereby the initial position of words assumes the most significant position in word recognition. Most of the words that children are initially asked to learn begin with consonant sounds.

23. Answers will vary.

24. As children begin to work with an increasing number of unknown polysyllabic words, they must be able to syllabicate them correctly first before applying vowel generalizations.

25. *Phonetics:* The scientific study of human speech sounds.

    Grapheme: A letter or combination of letters that represents a phoneme.

    Vowels: Sounds represented by *a, e, i, o, u,* and sometimes *y* and *w*.

    Diphthong: A single vowel sound made up of a glide from one vowel to another in immediate sequence and pronounced in one syllable.

    Consonant blend: Sounds in a syllable represented by two or more letters that are blended together without losing their own identities.

    Rime: The part of a syllable that includes the vowel sound and any consonant sound(s) that come(s) after it.

    Schwa: An unstressed sound commonly occurring in unstressed syllables. It closely resembles the sound of a short *u*.

CHAPTER 8: PRACTICE

1. Diagnostic teaching is the process whereby teachers identify students' strengths and weaknesses through both formal and informal means and use this diagnostic information to direct their instructional actions.

2. Unless teachers have diagnostic information to assist in the identification of the strengths and weaknesses of students, it is extremely difficult to set up instructional programs that allow students the opportunity to grow to their full potential.

3. a. Phoneme blending is the process of recognizing isolated speech sounds and the ability to pronounce the word for which they stand when combined.

   b. Phoneme segmentation is the ability to isolate all the sounds of a word.

4. a. Diagnosis should be viewed as a daily occurrence. Diagnosis is too often treated as a special event that takes place only once or twice a year. In reality, teachers need to observe and evaluate children on a continuing basis because children's needs and/or skills can change drastically over a short period.

   b. Decisions about children should be based on diagnostic information collected from various sources. Instructional decisions about children should never be made on the basis of a single test or observation. Generally, the more diverse the data that teachers collect, the more useful the information.

   c. The identification of patterns of error should be emphasized when analyzing diagnostic information. If a type of error occurs in a pattern, greater confidence can be placed on the interpretation that the error is truly a problem for the child. When decisions are based on isolated errors, unneeded instruction and practice often follow.

d. Work on only one or two reading weaknesses at a time. Often, when diagnosing children who exhibit problems in reading, several weaknesses will be identified. If attempts are made to remediate all these weaknesses at once, it generally overwhelms the children and further frustrates their efforts to improve. Narrow the skills to be taught to the one or two that appear to create the most difficulty and remediate these before continuing with others that are less debilitating.

e. Diagnosis for its own sake is not acceptable; it must lead to specific instructional action. Teachers must avoid becoming so enamored of the diagnostic process that they lose sight of the ultimate objective of diagnosis: the identification and remediation of weaknesses or disabilities.

CUMULATIVE REVIEW: CHAPTERS 1 TO 8

a. Phonics: A method in which basic phonetics, the study of human speech sounds, is used to teach beginning reading. Teachers teach phonics, not phonetics.

b. Phonetics: The study of human speech sounds.

c. Phoneme: The smallest *sound* unit of a language that distinguishes one word from another. Examples: the phoneme /h/ distinguishes *hat* from *at*; the words *tell* and *yell* are distinguished by their initial phonemes /t/ and /y/. (This text indicates that there are 44 phonemes in the American-English language. This number varies, however, according to different authorities and/or dialects. Slash marks, //, are used throughout the text to indicate that the reference is to a *sound* and not a *letter*.)

d. Phonemic Awareness: The ability to recognize spoken words as a sequence of individual sounds.

e. Consonant: A sound represented by any letter of the English alphabet except *a, e, i, o, u*. Consonants are sounds made by closing or restricting the breath channel.

f. Consonant Blend: Sounds in a syllable represented by two or more letters that are blended together without losing their own identities. Examples: blue /b/ /l/; gray /g/ /r/; brown /b/ /r/; twig /t/ /w/; street /s/ /t/ /r/; flip /f/ /l/.

g. Vowel: A sound represented by *a, e, i, o, u*, and sometimes *y* and *w*, in the English alphabet. Vowels are sounds made without closing or restricting the breath channel.

h. Diphthong: A single vowel sound made up of a glide from one vowel sound to another in immediate sequence and pronounced in one syllable. Examples: /oi/ in oil and boy; /ou/ in house and owl. (Phonetics would consider that some single-letter vowels represent diphthongs. For the purposes of teaching reading, however, only /oi/ and /ou/ will be considered diphthongs.)

i. R-Controlled Vowel: When a vowel letter is followed by the letter *r*, it affects the vowel sound so that it is neither short nor long. For example, in *her*, the vowel sound becomes /û/; in *dare*, it becomes /â/; in *for*, it becomes /ô/; in *car*, it becomes /ä/.

j. Schwa Sound: An unstressed sound commonly occurring in unstressed syllables. It is represented by the symbol /ə/ and closely resembles the short sound for *u*. Examples: *a* in *about; o* in *occur; i* in *pencil; u* in *circus*.

k. Grapheme: A letter or combination of letters that represents a phoneme (sound). Examples: the phoneme /b/ in *bat* is represented by the grapheme *b*; the phoneme /f/ in *phone* is represented by the grapheme *ph*. (There are over 200 different ways to spell the phonemes. For example, /f/ can take the form of *f* in *fine*, *gh* in *cough*, and *ph* in *elephant*. This is an example of three different graphemes representing the same phoneme.)

l. Digraph: Two letters that stand for a single phoneme (sound). Examples: thin /th/; each /ĕ/; shop /sh/; boy /oi/; look /ŏŏ/; rang /ng/; few /ōō/. A digraph is simply a grapheme of two letters.

m. Onset: The consonant sound(s) of a syllable that comes before the vowel sound. (Examples are included with the definition of *rime* below.)

n. Rime: The part of a syllable that includes the vowel sound and any consonant sound(s) that come(s) after it. The graphic representation of a rime is referred to as a *phonogram*. Following are examples of both onsets and rimes.

Word	Onset	Rime	Phonogram
mat	/m/	/at/	at
pig	/p/	/ig/	ig
at	—	/at/	at
split	/spl/	/it/	it

o. Phonogram: A letter sequence comprised of a vowel grapheme and an ending consonant grapheme(s), such as *-ig* in *wig, dig, big*, or the *-ack* in *back, tack, sack*. From phonograms we can generate word families.

p. Syllable: A unit of pronunciation consisting of a vowel alone or a vowel with one or more consonants. There can be only one vowel phoneme (sound) in each syllable.

q. Closed Syllable: Any syllable that ends with a consonant phoneme (sound). Examples: come /m/; paste /t/; love /v/; ran /n/.

r. Open Syllable: Any syllable that ends with a vowel sound (phoneme). Examples: see /ē/; may /ā/; boy /oi/; auto /ō/.

s. Breve: The orthographic symbol (˘) placed over a vowel letter to show it is pronounced as a short sound (sometimes called an unglided vowel).

t. Circumflex: The orthographic symbol (^) placed above vowel graphemes to indicate pronunciation.

u. Macron: The orthographic symbol (ˉ) placed over a vowel letter to show it is pronounced as a long sound (sometimes called a glided vowel).

v. Umlaut: The orthographic symbol (¨) placed above vowel graphemes to indicate pronunciation.

CHAPTER 9: PHONICS POST-TEST

1. Phonics
2. macron
3. digraph
4. closed
5. consonant blends
6. phoneme
7. diphthong
8. Graphemes
9. phonogram
10. Syllables
11. False
12. False
13. True
14. True
15. False
16. True
17. True
18. True
19. False
20. False
21. a
22. c
23. b
24. d
25. b
26. c
27. b
28. d
29. b
30. b

31. b
32. b
33. c
34. b
35. d
36. *digraph* refers to letters; the other terms refer to sounds.
37. *tw* represents a consonant blend; the others are consonant digraphs.
38. *boy* is the only word that contains letters that represent the diphthong sound.
39. *double* is the only word that does not contain letters representing the diphthong sound.
40. *cepp* is the only word that contains a "soft c."
41. 3,/b/ /l/ /o͞o/
42. 4,/h/ /û/ /r/ /d/
43. 6,/t/ /ŏ/ /k/ /s/ /ĭ/ /k/
44. 3,/sh/ /o͝o/ /d/
45. 2,/sh/ /o͞o/
46. 2,/â/ /r/
47. 4,/k/ /w/ /ĭ/ /t/
48. 5,/ă/ /n/ /t/ /ē/ /k/
49. 3,/s/ /ĕ/ /d/
50. 4,/s/ /k/ /o͞o/ /l/
51. b
52. c
53. b
54. a
55. c
56. b
57. a
58. c
59. c
60. c
61. a
62. d
63. a
64. a
65. d

66. b
67. b
68. S
69. L
70. S
71. L

GLOSSARY

accent (primary): The syllable in a word that receives the strongest and loudest emphasis.

analytic phonics: A whole-to-part phonics approach that emphasizes starting with whole words and identifying individual sounds as parts of those words. Efforts are generally made to avoid pronouncing letter sounds in isolation. Also known as *implicit phonics*.

auditory discrimination: The ability to hear similarities and differences between sounds as they occur in spoken words.

base word: A word to which prefixes and/or suffixes are added to create new but related words. The simplest member of a word family.

breve: An orthographic symbol, (˘), placed above vowel graphemes to indicate pronunciation.

circumflex: An orthographic symbol (ˆ) placed above vowel graphemes to indicate pronunciation.

closed syllable: Any syllable ending with a consonant phoneme. Examples: come /m/; love /v/; ran /n/.

compound word: A word made up of two or more base words.

consonant blend: Sounds in a syllable represented by two or more letters that are blended together without losing their own identity. Examples: blue /b/ /l/; brown /b/ /r/; twig /t/ /w/; street /s/ /t/ /r/; flip /f/ /l/.

consonants: Sounds represented by any letter of the English alphabet except *a, e, i, o,* and *u.* Consonants are *sounds* that are made by closing or restricting the breath channel.

decoding: The process of determining the pronunciation of an unknown word.

deductive instruction: Instructional procedure that centers on telling children about generalizations and having them apply the generalizations to specific words; a general-to-specific emphasis.

digraph: Two letters that stand for a single phoneme. Examples: thin /th/; each /ē/; shop /sh/; boy /oi/; look /o͝o/; rang /ng/; few/o͞o/. A digraph is simply a grapheme of two letters.

diphthong: A single vowel sound made up of a blend of two vowel sounds in immediate sequence and pronounced in one syllable. Examples: /oi/ in oil and boy; /ou/ in house and owl. (Phonetics would consider that some single-letter vowels are actually diphthongs. For the purposes of teaching reading, however, only /oi/ and /ou/ are considered diphthongs.)

grapheme: A letter or combination of letters that represents a phoneme. Examples: the phoneme /b/ in *bat* is represented by the grapheme *b*; the phoneme /f/ in *phone* is represented by the grapheme *ph*. There are over 200 different ways to spell the phonemes. For example, /f/ can take the form of *f* in *fine*, *gh* in *cough,* and *ph* in *elephant*, three different graphemes representing the same phoneme.

inductive instruction: Instructional procedure that begins with an analysis of specifics from which generalizations are formed; a specific-to-general emphasis.

macron: An orthographic symbol, (ˉ), placed over a vowel letter to show that it is pronounced as a long sound (sometimes called *glided vowels*).

onset: The consonant sound(s) of a syllable that comes before the vowel sound. (See the definition of *rime* for examples of *onsets*.)

open syllable: Any syllable ending with a vowel phoneme. Examples: see /ē/; may /ā/; boy /oi/; auto /ō/.

phoneme: The smallest *sound* unit of a language that distinguishes one word from another. Examples: The phoneme /h/ distinguishes *hat* from *at;* the words *tell* and *yell* are distinguished by their initial phonemes /t/ and /y/, respectively.

phoneme blending: The process of recognizing isolated speech sounds and the ability to pronounce the word for which they stand.

phoneme segmentation: The ability of isolating all the sounds of a word.

phonemic awareness: The ability to recognize spoken words as a sequence of individual sounds.

phonetics: The scientific study of human speech sounds.

phonics: A method in which basic phonetics, the study of human speech sounds, is used to teach beginning reading.

phonogram: A letter sequence comprised of a vowel grapheme and an ending consonant grapheme(s), such as *-ig* in *wig, dig,* and *big* or *-ack* in *back, tack,* and *sack.*

r-controlled vowel: When a vowel letter is followed by the letter *r*, it makes the vowel sound neither long nor short. For example, in *her,* the vowel sound becomes /û/; in *dare,* it becomes /â/.

rime: The part of a syllable that includes the vowel sound and any consonant sound(s) that comes after it. The graphic representation of a rime is referred to as a *phonogram.* For example, in the word *mat,* the onset is /m/, and the rime is /at/.

root: Often used as a synonym for *base word.*

schwa sound: An unstressed sound commonly occurring in unstressed syllables. It is represented by the symbol /e/, and it closely resembles the short sound for *u.* Examples: *a* in *about; o* in *occur; i* in *pencil; u* in *circus.*

syllable: A unit of pronunciation consisting of a vowel alone or a vowel with one or more consonants. There can be only one vowel phoneme (sound) in each syllable.

synthetic phonics: A part-to-whole phonics approach that emphasizes the learning of individual sounds, often in isolation, and combining them to form words. Also known as *explicit phonics.*

umlaut: An orthographic symbol, (¨), placed above vowel graphemes to indicate pronunciation.

visual discrimination: The ability to visually perceive similarities and differences (in reading, this means to perceive similarities and differences between written letters and words).

vowels: Sounds represented by *a, e, i, o, u,* and sometimes *y* and *w,* in the English alphabet. Vowels are sounds that are made without closing or restricting the breath channel.

REFERENCES AND RESOURCES

Adams, M. J. (1990). *Beginning to read: Thinking and learning about print.* Cambridge, MA: MIT Press.

Anderson, R. C., Hiebert, E. H., Scott, J. A., & Wilkinson, I. A. G. (1984). *Becoming a nation of readers: The report of the commission on reading.* Washington, DC: National Institute of Education, U.S. Department of Education.

Bailey, M. H. (1967, February). The utility of phonic generalizations in grades one through six. *The Reading Teacher, 20,* 413–418.

Bear, D., Invernizzi, M., Templeton, S., & Johnston, F. (2004). *Words their way* (3rd ed.). Upper Saddle River, NJ: Pearson.

Blackman, B. A. (1984, August). Relationship of rapid naming ability and language analysis skills to kindergarten and first-grade reading achievement. *Journal of Educational Psychology, 76,* 610–622.

Bond, G. L., & Dykstra, R. (1967). *Final report, project no. X-001.* Washington, DC: Bureau of Research, Office of Education, U.S. Department of Health, Education, and Welfare.

Bond, G. L., Tinker, M. A., Wasson, B. B., & Wasson, J. B. (1989). *Reading difficulties: Their diagnosis and correction* (6th ed.). Upper Saddle River, NJ: Merrill/Prentice Hall.

Bradley, L., & Bryant, P. E. (1983, February). Categorizing sounds and learning to read—A causal connection. *Nature, 301,* 419–421.

Burmeister, L. E. (1966). *An evaluation of the inductive and deductive group approaches to teaching selected word analysis generalizations to disabled readers in eighth and ninth grade.* Unpublished doctoral dissertation, University of Wisconsin.

Burmeister, L. E. (1968, February). Vowel pairs. *The Reading Teacher, 21,* 445–452.

Caldwell, E. C., Roth, S. R., & Turner, R. R. (1978, Spring). A reconsideration of phonic generalizations. *Journal of Reading Behavior, 10,* 91–96.

Caldwell, J., & Leslie, L. (2005). *Intervention strategies to follow informal reading inventory assessment.* Upper Saddle River, NJ: Pearson.

Calfee, R. C., Lindamood, P., & Lindamood, C. (1973, June). Acoustic-phonetic skills and reading—Kindergarten through twelfth grade. *Journal of Educational Psychology, 64,* 293–298.

Chall, J. (1967). *Learning to read: The great debate.* New York: McGraw-Hill.

Clymer, T. (1996, November). The utility of phonic generalizations in the primary grades. *The Reading Teacher, 50*(3), 182–187.

Durkin, D. (1993). *Teaching them to read* (6th ed.). Boston: Allyn & Bacon.

Edmiaston, R. K. (1984, July/August). Oral language and reading: How are they related for third graders? *Remedial and Special Education, 5,* 33–37.

Ehri, L. C. (1979). Linguistic insight: Threshold of reading acquisition. In T. G. Waller & G. E. MacKinnon (Eds.), *Reading research: Advances in theory and practice* (Vol. 1, pp. 63–114). New York: Academic Press.

Ekwall, E. (1976). *Diagnosis and remediation of the disabled reader.* Boston: Allyn & Bacon.

Emans, R. (1967, February). The usefulness of phonic generalizations above the primary grades. *The Reading Teacher, 20,* 419–425.

Emans, R. (1968, May). History of phonics. *Elementary English, 45,* 602–608.

Flavell, J. (1977). *Cognitive development.* Upper Saddle River, NJ: Merrill/Prentice Hall.

Flesch, R. (1955). *Why Johnny can't read.* New York: Harper Press.

Flynt, E., & Cooter, B. (2004). *Reading inventory for the classroom* (5th ed.). Upper Saddle River, NJ: Pearson.

Fox, B. (2003). *Word recognition activities patterns and strategies for developing fluency.* Upper Saddle River, NJ: Pearson.

Fuld, P. (1968, February). Vowel sounds in VCC words. *The Reading Teacher, 21,* 442–444.

Gates, L. (1986, Summer). The consonant generalizations revisited. *Reading Horizons, 26,* 232–236.

Golinkoff, R. M. (1978). Critique: Phonemic awareness skills and reading achievement. In F. B. Murray & L. L. Pikulski (Eds.), *The acquisition of reading: Cognitive linguistic, and perceptual prerequisites* (pp. 23–41). Baltimore: University Park Press.

Groff, P. J. (1984, January). Resolving the letter name controversy. *The Reading Teacher, 37,* 384–388.

Harris, L. A., & Smith, C. B. (1986). *Reading instruction: Diagnostic teaching in the classroom* (4th ed.). New York: Macmillan.

Heilman, A. W. (1981). *Phonics in proper perspective* (4th ed.). Upper Saddle River, NJ: Merrill/Prentice Hall.

Hillerich, R. L. (1978, April). Reading: Phonics—What about the rules? *Teacher, 95*(8), 94.

Houghton Mifflin. (1997a). *Family treasures* (Level 1.5 teacher's ed.). Boston: Author.

Houghton Mifflin. (1997b). *Try it my way* (Level 5 teacher's ed.). Boston: Author.

Houghton Mifflin. (1997c). *Unexpected guests* (Level 1.4 teacher's ed.). Boston: Author.

Johns, J. L. (1991). *Basic reading inventory* (5th ed.). Dubuque, IA: Kendall/Hunt.

Lewkowicz, N. K. (1980, October). Phonemic awareness training: What to teach and how to teach it. *Journal of Educational Psychology, 72,* 686–700.

Mann, V. (1994). Phonological skills and the prediction of early reading problems. In N. C. Jordan & J. Goldsmith-Phillips (Eds.), *Learning disabilities: New directions for assessment and intervention.* Needham Heights, MA: Allyn & Bacon.

Meyerson, M., & Kulesza, D. (2002). *Strategies for struggling readers step by step.* Upper Saddle River, NJ: Pearson.

Moats, L. (2000). *Speech to print. Language essentials for teachers.* Baltimore: Brookes.

Nation, A., & Hulme, C. (1997, April–June). Phonemic segmentation, not onset-rime segmentation, predicts early reading and spelling skills. *Reading Research Quarterly, 32,* 154–167.

National Institute of Child Health and Human Development. (2000a). Report of the National Reading Panel. *Teaching children to read: An evidence-based assessment of the scientific research literature on reading and its implications for reading instruction* (NIH Publication No. 00-4769). Washington, DC: U.S. Government Printing Office.

National Institute of Child Health and Human Development. (2000 b). Report of the Subgroups of the National Reading Panel. *Teaching children to read: An evidence-based assessment of the scientific research literature on reading and its implications for reading instruction* (NIH Publication No. 00-4754). Washington, DC: U.S. Government Printing Office.

Rosenthal, A. S., Baker, K., & Ginsburg, A. (1983, October). The effects of language background on achievement level and learning among elementary school students. *Sociology of Education, 56,* 157–169.

Searfoss, L. W., & Readence, J. E. (1994). *Helping children learn to read* (3rd ed.). Boston: Allyn & Bacon.

Shanker, J., & Ekwall, E. (2003). *Locating and correcting reading difficulties* (8th ed.). Upper Saddle River, NJ: Pearson.

Silvaroli, N. J. (1994). *Classroom reading inventory* (7th ed.). Dubuque, IA: Brown & Benchmark.

Silver Burdett Ginn. (1993). *Make a wish* (Level 1.5 teacher's ed.). Needham, MA: Author.

Smith, F. (1982). *Understanding reading* (3rd ed.). New York: Holt, Rinehart and Winston.

Snow, C. E., Burns, M. S., & Griffin, P. (Eds.). (1998). *Preventing reading difficulties in young children.* Washington, DC: National Academy Press.

Spache, G. D., Andres, M. C., Curtis, H. A., Rowland, M. L., & Fields, M. H. (1965). *A longitudinal first-grade reading readiness program* (Cooperative Research Project No. 2742). Tallahassee: Florida State Department of Education.

Spache, G. D., & Spache, E. B. (1986). *Reading in the elementary school* (5th ed.). Boston: Allyn & Bacon.

Stahl, S. A., Osborn, J., & Lehr, F. (1990). *Beginning to read: Thinking and learning about print—A summary.* University of Illinois at Urbana–Champaign; Center for the Study of Reading, Reading Research and Education Center.

Stuart, M. (1999). Getting ready for reading: Early phoneme awareness and phonics teaching improves reading and spelling in inner-city second language learners. *British Journal of Educational Psychology, 69,* 587–605.

Sulzby, E., & Teale, W. (1991). Emergent literacy. In R. Barr, M. L. Kamil, P. B. Mosenthal, & P. D. Pearson (Eds.), *Handbook of reading research* (Vol. 2, pp. 727–757). New York: Longman.

Swearingen, R., & Allen, D. (2000). *Classroom assessment of reading processes* (2nd ed.). Boston: Houghton Mifflin.

Thorndike, E. L., & Lorge, I. (1944). *The teacher's word book of 30,000 words.* New York: Bureau of Publications, Teachers College, Columbia University.

Trelease, J. (1995). *The new read-aloud handbook* (3rd ed.). New York: Viking Penguin.

Tunmer, W. E., & Nesdale, A. R. (1985, August). Phonemic segmentation skill and beginning reading. *Journal of Educational Psychology, 77*, 417–427.

Walker, B. (2005). *Techniques for reading assessment and instruction.* Upper Saddle River, NJ: Pearson.

Woods, M. L., & Moe, A. J. (2003). *Analytical reading inventory* (7th ed.). Upper Saddle River, NJ: Prentice Hall.

Wylie, R. E., & Durrell, D. D. (1970). Teaching vowels through phonograms. *Elementary English, 47*, 787–791.

ADDITIONAL WEB-BASED RESOURCES

Audio Sites
http://www.antimoon.com/how/pronunc-soundsipa.htm

Audio Sites with Links
http://www.sunburstmedia.com/PronWeb.html
http://www.uiowa.edu/~acadtech/phonetics/english/frameset.html
http://dictionary.reference.com/search?q=speech

Center for Applied Linguistics
http://www.cal.org/

Consonant Blends/Digraph Activities
http://www.phonicsworld.com/Consonantblends.html
http://www.tampareads.com/phonics/whereis/index.htm

Consonants
http://evaeaston.com/pr/consonants.html

**DIBELS (Dynamic Indicators of Basic Early Literacy Skills)
Home Page**
http://dibels.uoregon.edu/

Diphthongs
http://www.sadlier-oxford.com/phonics/grade2_3/dipthongs/dipthongs.htm
http://www.celt.stir.ac.uk/staff/HIGDOX/STEPHEN/PHONO/VOWEL/
    DIPH.HTM

ERIC Linking Site to Educational Information
http://bcol01.ed.gov/CFAPPS/ERIC/resumes/descriptorsummary.cfm?majo
    rdesc=Basal%20Reading

Evaluations of Basal Series
http://www.auburn.edu/~murraba/evaluation.html

Four Blocks
http://teachers.net/gazette/APR03/sigmon.html

General Information on Worldwide Use of Diacritical Marks
http://www.businessballs.com/diacriticalmarks.htm

Great Vowel Shift
http://alpha.furman.edu/~mmenzer/gvs/what.htm

International Phonetic Alphabet
http://www.omniglot.com/writing/ipa.htm
http://www.arts.gla.ac.uk/IPA/ipachart.html

International Reading Association Home Page
http://www.reading.org/

Merriam-Webster Dictionary
http://www.m-w.com

National Council of Teachers of English (NCTE)
http://www.ncte.org/

The Oxford English Dictionary
http://www.oed.com/

Phonograms
http://www.literacyconnections.com/Phonograms.html
http://www.phonogrampage.com/

Resources for Spoken English
http://faculty.washington.edu/dillon/PhonResources/PhonResources.html

Roots and Prefixes
http://www.quia.com/jg/66094.html
http://www.edhelper.com/Word_Roots.htm
http://ancienthistory.about.com/library/weekly/aa052698.htm

Syllabication by Grade-Level Activities
http://www.edhelper.com/language/Syllabication.htm
http://www.createdbyteachers.com/syllablerulescharts.html
http://www.spelling.org/free/syllabication_rules.htm
http://english.glendale.cc.ca.us/SYLLABLES.html

Schwa
http://englishplus.com/grammar/00000383.htm

Schwa Links—Technical
http://www.reference.com/browse/wiki/Schwa

Short Vowel Sounds
http://rbeaudoin333.homestead.com/shortvowel_1.html
http://www.learninghaven.com/la/spelling/short_vowel_sounds.htm
http://www.readingkey.com/phonics/sounds/vowels/voweltest.htm

Sight Word Resources
http://www.fcboe.org/schoolhp/shes/sight_words.htm
http://literacyconnections.com/Dolch.html
http://www.createdbyteachers.com/sightfreemain.html

Speech and Special Education
http://parentpals.com/gossamer/pages/Speech_and_Language/Articulation
_and_Phonology/

Speech Articulation
http://academic.gallaudet.edu/pages/A&S/james.mahshie/714/articulation-
vowels/index.htm

Typing Diacritical Marks for Composing Activities in the Classroom
http://www.power-glide.com/newsletter/e-correo/archive/volume02_issue17
/howtotype.html